ENGLISH PARISH CHURCHES

ENGLISH PARISH CHURCHES

ENGLISH
PARISH CHURCHES

TEXT BY GRAHAM HUTTON

226 PHOTOGRAPHS BY

EDWIN SMITH

LONDON

THAMES AND HUDSON

TEXT PRINTED IN GREAT BRITAIN BY JARROLD AND SONS LIMITED NORWICH
GRAVURE PLATES PRINTED BY CLARKE AND SHERWELL LIMITED NORTHAMPTON

ENGLISH PARISH CHURCHES

THE parish churches of England epitomize English history and the English way of life better than any other institution. Collectively, they are a national storehouse of architectural and artistic beauty. On the European Continent parish churches are recognizable children of cathedrals, which they closely resemble. English parish churches are not. They have developed on their own, as things apart, of the people themselves, of the village and—much later—of the town: as parts of everyday English existence, of secular as well as religious use from the outset. Parish churches are the oldest—because they were the first—communal buildings in English history; and every change in that history—social, cultural, military and religious—is reflected in them.

English cathedrals are a glorious architectural and artistic *tour de force;* but they do not tell a comparable story. They are restricted to four centuries. The churches rove through thirteen. Englishmen tend to find their cathedrals, as Dr. Hürlimann emphasized in a companion volume to this, "strange and foreign". But their parish churches are familiar parts of the social fabric; they both reflect and express the English way of life; and it is no accident that England's literature and parish churches have been intimately associated from their dim beginnings. In those two manifestations of national temperament and character, English genius, too, is seen at its purest and most effective. Before the churches arose, there were "standing crosses" where the Word was preached or the Mass celebrated by itinerant missionary priests, members of our earliest bishops' *familiae.* On the magnificent specimen at Ruthwell, in Scotland, are graven some of the first lines in English literature: Cynewulf's *Dream of the Rood,* which some attribute to Caedmon himself.

*

Among a city-hating, heathen, agricultural people—properly called *pagani*—arose arts and crafts, a missionary zeal, an enthusiasm for classical literature and Christian learning, and a sense of practical administration, all of which were to impress the name of the English upon Continental Europe. The conversion of the "Germans" by Winfrith (St. Boniface), the spreading of the fame of Northumbria's royal St. Oswald across the Continent into Italy along the line of churches named after him, the organization of the Carolingian Renaissance, the widespread influence of English clerks and artists: these were but repayments in kind for earlier loans of learning and art which—in the hands of Augustine, Paulinus, Theodore, or of anonymous Syrians, Copts, Gauls and other masons, sculptors and artists—the dying Roman world had made to the first Englishmen.

The invaders of the Roman Empire on the Continent—with the possible exception of the Saxons on the northern French coast and the Vandals in their short passage from Spain to Africa—went by land. There was a *limes*, a threshold, a frontier of the Roman world with traffic or trade across it; once these Continental invaders had destroyed the frontier, they adopted what they found beyond it, and conformed to what they had always feared, admired or emulated. That is what happened to Visigoths in Spain and Gaul, Franks and Burgundians in Gaul, Ostrogoths and Lombards in Italy. They lost their original languages, religions, tribal organizations and folk-arts. They adopted those of the Christian Roman provincials. They adopted their cities, provincial boundaries, agricultural methods, even their titles and social gradations.

But none of that happened in England. Here, the barbarian invaders took over 150 years to occupy "Saxon" England alone. They overthrew the remnants of the former Romano-British system, which had already disintegrated, and pressed what was left of it westward; they brought in their own methods, refused Christianity, avoided cities, broke new ground and settled new communities on it. They had been in England for its two darkest centuries—still both heathen and pagan—when Augustine landed in Kent in 597. They were more of one kind by the seventh century than were the still fermenting peoples of those kingdoms which were later to become France, Germany, Italy and Spain.

It is important to bear the remote heathen past in mind when considering the Church of England, and when viewing any English rural parish church; for the "parish" itself in most of England—as contrasted with Continental parishes—has a different origin. So have most of England's villages and manors, and most of her big cities. So have the dioceses of the older English bishoprics, which still show the boundaries of the original Saxon kingdoms, whereas those of the Continent show those of Roman provinces.

Even the still persistent strongholds of British Puritanism and Nonconformity—the originally Celtic lands of Wales, Devon, Dorset, Somerset, Cornwall, and Scotland—are to some extent explicable in terms of this dim, heathen *English* past. For these were the lands of the Celtic, Roman-British church, which went from Britain to Ireland in the person of St. Patrick, and to Scotland and Northumbria in the persons of Ninian, Columba, and Aidan. The Celtic church was one of travelling monks; of modest ritual and simple souls. Such men found Augustine of Rome "arrogant" when he first met their representatives. Yet the Celtic Church had to bow to the Roman rite at Whitby in 663-4 and leave Northumbria. Many of the folk in those Celtic parts of England and of Britain never wholly "took to" the Church of England and its episcopal organization, as later established. More of them, as time went on, were to leave it altogether, and become Nonconformists.

So far in time—and yet so near among us today, among Baptists, Methodists, Presbyterians and other Nonconformists, members of the Episcopal Church of England, Roman Catholics, agnostics and atheists, all of us—are the shadowy figures of Patrick of Ireland, Ninian and Columba of Scotland, Augustine of Kent, Aidan and Paulinus of Northumbria, Birinus of Wessex, Cedd of Essex, Chad of Mercia, and the wise and

6

cultured Theodore of Tarsus who first organized the Christian church of all England about the year 670.

That happens to be the year to which two of the first churches portrayed in this book are ascribed: Brixworth (14 and 19)* and Escomb (3); the one in Southumbrian Mercia, the other in Northumbria, the two main divisions of the English church and its people.

*

Professor R. H. Hodgkin, in *A History of the Anglo-Saxons* (Oxford, 1935) says, "Perhaps the most important development which went on unobtrusively within the Church in the eighth century—as also in earlier and later times—was the gradual formation of the parish system." This system took shape from the missionary work, which radiated from the centres of the dioceses where the first "cathedral churches" were built; also from the building of churches by the heathen and Christian landowners for their folk, or for a body of clergy who settled among them and prevailed on them to grant land or materials, or both, for the good of their own and others' souls. So from the Conversion to the Conquest, three kinds of churches gradually emerged: (1) the early diocesan "cathedral churches"; (2) the later "collegiate churches"; and (3) the local *thegns'* private chapels and true prototypes of the modern parish church. The first kind—Bishop Cedd's lovely grey-stone barn at Bradwell-juxta-Mare in Essex is one of the few remaining examples—were known as "mother churches", since from these the first missionaries had radiated Christianity throughout the first dioceses. The second kind—the collegiate churches, monasteries, etc.—were known as "old minsters" (*monasteria*) because of their early collegiate foundation. The third kind—as diverse at the outset as they are now—were first referred to as "churches" or chapels, but later became known as "parish churches". They "belonged" to *thegns*, bishops, private colleges and "new minsters" (which were later foundations than the "old minsters") and finally, to lay corporations or associations of parishioners and the like.

The English parish is of uncertain origin. The word comes from the civil administration of the ancient world, where it meant something like a province. When first applied to the early church in England, it meant the territory of a bishop—what we would now call a diocese (which is also a word taken from the administrative system of the ancient world). Some parishes today, in parts of England where population was and still is sparse, contain a number of villages; whereas most cities and towns have slowly split into a number of parishes. Blackstone thought parish boundaries came from those of an original manor. He may have been right. The manor was naturally the ultimate territorial unit under the Saxons' agricultural organization, for they avoided Britain's ancient cities while they were heathens. It was not until after the Danish troubles, in the last 150 years before the Norman Conquest, that real towns rose again in England.

Under both the heathen and the converted Saxons, the Church was a rural affair. It depended on tithes and other offerings, which generally went to the bishop and his adminis-trative officers. The fourth Council of Orleans as early as 541 decreed that if anyone built a church, it should be endowed with land or sustenance so that a priest could serve it. But in

* Throughout this book, numbers in brackets refer to the Plates and the corresponding Notes

England the parish church, with *its own* priest and particular income, was not a settled and general institution until about the Norman Conquest; it was then that the parishes and churches of towns and cities really began to multiply. For four centuries before that, the local church, priest and congregation were all part and parcel of the local Saxon lordship, manor, or manors. One of the later ways of becoming a *thegn* or Saxon lord was to build a church, especially a church with a tower. (It may well have been for civil defences during the Danish wars; and it may be that at this time began the peculiarly English style of parish church with western tower and side entrances.) From the very beginnings of Saxon Christianity the territorial lord could build a local church, put in his own priest, endow it (and him), change him for another, sell or otherwise transfer or bequeath "his" church, and even take it to pieces and make a mill or house out of it somewhere else—which was easier to do when churches in thickly forested England were mainly of wood, as they were until after the struggle with the Danes.

In all parts of England, therefore, the local or "parish" church arose in an everyday setting of everyday relationships between all sorts and conditions of neighbourly and often kindred men. It had both religious and secular uses. It was the church of the common folk and their immediate lord, a family affair, an essential element of daily life, the first communal building in our history. So developed the church of that ultimate unit in England's local government, in England's rough-and-ready democracy: the parish. So it remains, in rural England, today. The parish church of town and city came later, it belongs to another age, another form of society. And to this day England's different historical epochs go on living around us in these several kinds of churches.

*

For eyes which know what to look for, there is perhaps more to see in the parish churches of England than in those of any other country. Through the centuries, the social and ritual changes had their effect on architectural and other styles. From early days the chancel of a parish church belonged to the rector; it was his duty to maintain it. The nave was the people's portion, the place of the parishioners, for which they were generally responsible. This had curious results. It is not only because of the shortage of good local stone for quoins that so many of the earlier Norfolk and Suffolk churches have a good stone or stone-reinforced chancel, and a flint-walled nave and western *round* tower. It is also because the parishioners or other lay authorities had to build the nave and tower, and flints were more common and cheaper. So was round, instead of squared, work.

Up to the Reformation the English parish church was generally plastered over within and often, in the case of the smaller churches, without. Its inside walls had edifying single- or many-coloured stories in pictures painted on them for an illiterate congregation. Paulinus of Nola in the fourth, and Bishop St. Apollinaris Sidonius in the fifth century, tell us that it kept crude minds off other subjects. In the case of the larger churches all statuary—whether inside the building or out—on tombs, rood-screens, etc., was painted in rich colours. We can scarcely visualize how splendid a parish church must have seemed to its parishioners, who, wresting a poor living from the soil, had leisure forced upon them not only by the changing seasons, but through the incidence of saints' days, war, sickness and festivals. The best which the local lord and the rest of the laity could offer would find its way to the church. It is reasonable to assume that from the beginnings of Christianity in Saxon England until the renaissance at the end of the Norman period in 1189—that is, for the six centuries of agrarian feudalism and restricted trade—the Church in all its forms must have absorbed at least one-third of the economic effort and output of the country, and perhaps one-half: in buildings of all kinds (not churches alone), skills, crafts, agricultural produce, metals, textiles, the arts, and so on.

We marvel today that so many churches came to be built, so swiftly, so durably, by so much free labour, and in so communal a spirit all over the land. We marvel at the magnificence of those that remain among us. Yet they are but pale, sad shadows of their pristine selves. Inside most of them the plaster, with its many-coloured patterns and pictures, has gone. In its place are walls of drab grey stone or, worse, of cement, making all dull and cold (46, 86, and 126); there are only a few instances today to show how bright a church can be with new plaster and white or washed walls (224). In most cases the plaster has gone from the outside walls, too, leaving the flints, rubble, bricks or stones exposed to the elements, and the gaunt quoins sticking out to show where the plastered surface of each wall once ran (23 and 27). The statuary and carving without and within—on western fronts or in porches and over portals, in niche or on buttress, on screen or tomb, on capital or font—have not been painted for centuries: in most cases not since the Protestant majority of our reforming ancestors—or the unaesthetic and arrogant minority of Puritans a century later—levied war upon graven images and laid them low. So today we see them only as through a glass, darkly: fractured or savagely chiselled across; when left intact by men, worn away by the wind and rain, by frost or sulphur fumes; and sometimes, even when restored with good intent and taste, restored with the wrong stone and without paint. It therefore needs something of the poet's eye to see them as they must have been. Nevertheless, he would be dull indeed who could see mere stonework or old paint in the ravaged or despoiled Saxon roods of Chichester, Langford (15), and Breamore; the simple Saxon Virgin of Inglesham (11) and the Christ Majesty of Barnack (12); the rood-screens of Ludham (145), Southwold (128), and Bramfield (106); the font of Trunch (138), the shrine of St. Wite (72), or the columns and capitals of West Walton (73) and Faringdon (84). A seeing eye will clothe these bones with what they once wore, and wore so bravely.

It is right to recognize the continuous indebtedness of Englishmen to Continental European architects and artists. As we saw, the initial Continental, and even Asiatic or African, impulses in architecture and the arts—particularly sculpture—found fertile soil in early Christian England. That set of influences was reinforced by the motifs and mythology of the Vikings. The next impulse was the Carolingian and post-Carolingian, chiefly Rhenish, which declared itself mainly in baluster-shafts, "long-and-short" work, stone stripwork, and the strange triangular heads to doors and windows (16). Then this, too, was developed by Englishmen along lines of their own, until the Norman wave of architectural and artistic influence broke over England. This in turn gave way to a Transitional flamboyance, a reassertion of some native English motifs, and the beautiful English version of Ile de France Gothic known as Early English. From the time of the Decorated period onward—throughout the Gothic periods to the renaissance of Classical styles in England (beginning with Tudor and Jacobean)—out-standing Continental artists of all kinds were continuously coming to England, drawn by the

B
9

growing prosperity of the big towns. To them we owe the motifs—but not the craftsmanship—of the fine English alabaster tombs (173); the revival of mosaic, inlaid marble panelling, strip-work of all kinds in monuments, and a continuous urge towards masterly sculpture.

Now let us consider the broad lines of development in each of the major periods of our parish church history; the Saxon, Norman, Gothic (Transitional and Early English, Decorated, Perpendicular and Tudor), Renaissance and Classical, and Gothic Revival. This, we hope, will help the reader to "place" the various churches in the series of photographs that follows, and which constitutes the major part of this volume.

The very plan and shape of the English parish church vary with time and place. The Saxon churches in the south, inspired by the Augustinian and other Roman missions, partake of the classical basilican form, mainly with aisles, western portals, eastern apses and no tran-septs: the churches at Wing (23), Brixworth (19), and Worth (4, 20) are typical examples, while the ruins of the Roman-British church at Silchester, Hampshire, the earliest known in England, still has its apse to the west. In the north, inspired by the Celtic missions, the earliest churches were far simpler: plain, tall, narrow, rectangular cells with side portals, having at best a small sanctuary at the square east end and possibly a lateral *porticus* (a primitive transept) or two. Such a porticus can be seen at Breamore (5), and Bradford-on-Avon (1). Strangely enough, it was the northern type, the more severe, with its rectangular east end to the chancel, which superseded the southern basilican form and survived as the prototype of most English parish churches—though it was the southern or Roman rite and cult which overcame and survived those of the Celtic church.

On the Continent of Europe the original basilican east end, the apse, persisted right through the Gothic period. In England, few parish churches retained the apsidal east end, the sanctuary being generally rectangular with a window or windows facing east. So the visitor of today, when he encounters an apsidal east end, as at Kilpeck (36) or Hales (35), will probably be struck by this feature. Already at Escomb (3), and Bradford-on-Avon (2), the sanctuary has a rectangular east end. With this Celtic and Anglian angularity goes the per-sistent English preference for lateral entrances and porches, generally on the south side, and for the tower at the west end (from middle Saxon times this was preferred); there is a corre-sponding absence of the majestic and complex western portals and façades of Continental parish churches. Several English parish churches of this Continental kind were built, it is true, in every period—for instance, Brixworth (14) in Saxon times; Iffley (31), Stewkley (52), and Mel-bourne (46) in Norman days; Ketton (80) in the Transitional and Early English epoch: and Higham Ferrers even later. But in England the western entrance has mainly been reserved for cathedrals and big collegiate churches. The English parish church generally presents a more modest mien to the outside world, and its lateral porches came to have a much greater secular significance—for trade, law, civil administration, and even military matters—than the imposing and ornamental west fronts of Continental churches.

In England the crypt proper—the raised chancel with the saint's relics in the *confessio* below, visible from the nave and half-buried in the earth, as in the earliest Italian and other Continental churches—disappears early. The only early example left in England is at Wing (23). Wilfred's crypts at Ripon and Hexham remain, but were not of this original basilican kind. They, like all other early so-called crypts in England, are completely subterranean places of worship, burial, or safe-keeping for relics.

The four dark centuries of Saxon England are in many ways the most fascinating part of parish church history. Few native Englishmen or visitors realize that there are from 1,500 to 2,500 Anglo-Saxon monuments, most of them in stone, still standing in or near our churches. In Yorkshire alone there are over 500. Saxon church-building is represented by three styles: the southern, mainly Italian-inspired, due to Augustine's mission; the northern, mainly inspired from Gaul; and mid-way, mainly in Mercia, a mixture of the two. These three styles are naturally seen at their clearest at the very beginnings of Christian building, in the seventh to ninth centuries, before the Danish invasions. In the north stands the well-coursed, high and narrow stone church of Escomb (3), which in all probability Benedict Biscop built with the aid of Gaulish masons in or about the year 700. In contrast with it is the vast, broad basilica of Mercian Brixworth (14, 19), built of stone, Roman bricks and tufa some thirty years earlier on the site of both a Roman and a heathen temple, by indirect inspiration of the Kentish missionaries and their workers.

In terms of art and craftsmanship, the centuries before the Danish invasions offer us finer work than those that followed—for instance, that unique English contribution to the early sculptures of Europe, the Anglian crosses. There is no figure-sculpture like it in Europe between the seventh and the twelfth centuries. Josef Strzygowski says in his *Origin of Christian Church Art* (tr. Oxford, 1923), "We may say at once of Anglo-Saxon works of art that they create an impression of spontaneity and freshness as enduring as that produced by the works of early Greek or early Gothic art. . . . Whether I turn to the remains of Anglo-Saxon churches, to the crosses, or to the MSS of the time of Bede, I feel in the presence of an art which differs from every other art in the world." The impulse for these carved crosses seems to have come from Theodore's Syria, or Abbot Adrian's Africa (then falling beneath the sword of Islam), by way of still-Byzantine Rome and Ravenna. The teacher must have been from the Hellenistic Orient; but he had English pupils of remarkable aptitude. Something of the initial Alexandrian purity of the work can still be seen at Britford (9), the vine-scroll appearing much as it does in sixth-century Ravenna or Constantinople; but by the later "time of troubles" heathen Scandinavian impulses are superimposed (10); and in figure-sculpture the earlier, deeper work yields to shallower Scandinavian kinds, as at Kirkby Stephen (8) or Middleton-by-Pickering (13). There are few more intriguing quests than the attempt to trace the degeneration of this earliest of our national expressions of genius under the impact of Danes, Vikings and Norsemen.

This dark Saxon era, however, displayed extraordinary variety and initiative; compare the crude and pathetic but forceful village-type of Virgin and Child at Inglesham (11) with the stern suavity of the later rood-figure at Langford (15). Or contrast the lively Roman brickwork of the triangular-headed door in the Italianate tower of Holy Trinity, Colchester (24) with the magnificent strip-and-pilaster work and carvings on the towers of Earls Barton and Barnack. It is from the Saxon towers—outside, with their distinctive stripwork or baluster-shafts, and inside, with their vast arches—that we also gain an idea of the tough simplicity of the first Englishmen (21). A people whose builders re-used Roman bricks and stones, as in the chancel-arch at Escomb or the votive stone at Tunstall (7), and could leave us as notable a Christ-Majesty as that of Barnack (12), or a Danish door as massive as that of Hadstock (6), were resourceful and versatile.

One striking aspect of the Norman Conquest was the way in which—for all its architectural, administrative, legal and ecclesiastical reforms and improvements—it achieved uniformity at the cost of temporarily suppressing the individual versatility and non-conformability of the Englishmen. Yet those very "non-conforming" characteristics break out, again and again, under the Normans themselves. We think the Avebury font (45) was carved, perhaps to Norman designs, by a Saxon. When Norman Romanesque has in its turn yielded to the French Gothic under the hands of Cluniac and Cistercian and other Orders, native originality emerges again in Early English, to reach an almost everyday virtuosity in the rich and unique Perpendicular style which made English church architecture famous.

On the Continent, in the main, the parish church and the cathedral have much in common: in plan, style, decoration, fittings. This, too, comes in part from the greater Continental continuity since Roman times. It has not been so in England, from the time when our first bishops, under Theodore's guidance, began to "oversee" their dioceses, organize parishes, and agree with local lords to allow the latter to build churches. When the Normans began their great work of unification in England, they found themselves faced with a bewilderingly various, random, sporadic, and intensely parochial English church, which they could only really subordinate to a broad pattern in the south and east of their newly won land. Different Norman churches, of a few well-marked grades and sizes, arose on all sides; on all sides most of the rougher, yet more various, Anglo-Saxon churches—and their lovelier contents—disappeared. Within fifty to seventy-five years of 1066, however, both the Anglo-Norman cathedrals or abbeys and the smaller churches—minster or parish—begin to show many more individual, local and other variations than do contemporary churches in Normandy.

The plan and shape of the English parish church, therefore, altered and varied more under the Normans. To begin with, they destroyed or radically restored many Saxon churches, and built anew and more massively. They gave us aisleless cruciform churches, with a central tower and transepts (Stow, 33, and Old Shoreham, 50, 56); aisleless churches without transepts but with a central tower (Iffley, 31, 34, Stewkley, 52); aisled churches with and without transepts, some going back to the basilican model (Melbourne, 46); fine small churches without tower, aisles, transepts or choir, but with rectangular chancels (Barfreystone, 37); and even aisleless, towerless churches with nave, central section (choir) and apsidal chancel (Kilpeck, 36). The lateral Saxon-style porches were generally retained in Norman England as entrances, as were some western towers (Sompting, 16).

The Normans brought light into the English parish church—windows with glass in them, therefore more and bigger windows, and the triforium and clerestory in the larger churches. They brought more complex piers, columns, capitals and—most strikingly—stone vaulting. They also brought (perhaps because of the Cistercians) the first strong dose of ecclesiastical severity, even austerity, for Englishmen to swallow. The old Saxon walls, covered inside with pictures, symbols and carvings, gave way to more severe patterning and picking out, or received manuscript-like drawings and pictures of a formal kind. Carving degenerated sadly. Striking

12

as most Norman doorways, tympana, corbel-tables and capitals seem (we show too many to name them separately), it is not until a century after the Conquest that the spirit of the individual and English sculptor begins once more to be discernible. And then, significantly, it does so away in the Welsh Marches where some unknown and un-Norman artist had a school, strongly impregnated with old Scandinavian motifs, near Kilpeck (40).

Norman ecclesiastical reorganization went far and deep. The systematic side of it is everywhere apparent: for example, in the number of standardized fonts, either of lead, showing the seasons and months and their labours (43, and 71), or of imported or local stone in various types and schools from Cornwall (151) to the Roman wall. Here, perhaps, and in odd unexpected places—see the swastikas at Great Canfield (41)—the native Saxon or Danish sculptors and carvers kept up their craft, within the limitations of Norman design. Yet sometimes individuality blazes out, as in the famous wall-paintings at Chaldon (55) and Great Canfield, and in those which once adorned the chancel at Barfreystone. Under the Normans, too, four of England's five round churches came into being, the fifth (at Little Maplestead) being of the fourteenth century. That of the Temple in London was lost in the recent war, but those of the Holy Sepulchre at Northampton and Cambridge (49) remain in service. That at Ludlow is a ruin.

The Norman contribution was great. It was a kind of renaissance. Yet there was something too massive, ponderous, austere and static about its church architecture; not the austerity of the high, narrow, dim-lighted, and relatively slender-walled Saxon buildings, but that of efficient-minded men working to strict plans, cautious over stresses, making their walls thicker than any England has ever seen, still hesitating to try proper buttresses, and unable to compass a flying-buttress to support a stone-vaulted roof. But, with all this hesitancy and working-to-rule, it was under the Normans that bricks and tiles were again used in England for walls, arches and floors; that triforia and clerestories at least suggested the need for vaulted roofs buttressed from without; that glass, screens and general ornamentation were made necessary parts of the parish church; and that the first stone vaults, corbels and pointed arches made a transition to the Early English style.

*

The Gothic styles further varied the plan and shape of the English parish church. It is worth quoting Dr. Cox's famous dictum on our parish churches: "collectively . . . England's most characteristic contribution to Gothic art". Many Gothic-seeming parish churches are reared upon Norman arcades (Walsoken, 47, 137); and some (Wing 23, Bibury, 60, 194, Avebury, 27, 45) show every style from Saxon to Tudor and later, in a kind of stately progression throughout the structure. It was in the three or four centuries of Gothic building, between 1150 and 1550, that the many local variations of ground-plan and style developed in English parish churches; the throwing-out of new aisles to accommodate a population which, until 1348, was growing steadily; the earlier equal, or almost equal, nave and aisles of East Anglia, with a fine long run of clerestory to light the splendid timbered roofs; the much later equal, or almost equal, nave and aisles of Devon, Cornwall and the West Country, without clerestory, mainly with barrel-vaulted or gabled separate roofs to nave and aisles; the timber churches of the Welsh Marches and Cheshire (Lower Peover, 176, 177, showing a Gothic interior in late Tudor times); the first new brick churches of East Anglia, and Essex in particular (though some, like East Guldeford, 178, 179, are in the south) also in Tudor times; the continued use of local flint, in rubble or with stone as a whimsical surface flushwork, in East Anglia; and the beautiful variety of local stones, from Yorkshire, Lincolnshire and the Northamptonshire region across England, through Oxfordshire, Warwickshire and Cotswold Gloucestershire, to Wiltshire, Dorset and Somerset in the south-west, ending with the red sandstone of Devon and the dark or polychrome granite of Cornwall.

Let the reader at this point look back through the photographs of Saxon and Norman churches, and then forward for only a few pages of plates: he will see at once that something light, expansive, and venturesome—yet severely functional—has happened, as a result of which there will be less need, from now on, to fill out the photographs with explanatory matter. Uffington church (64, 67) makes a good start; it contains many original features: the triangular-gabled chapels (67) with their lancet lights, the portal and its gable, the enormous increase in window-space. Even more striking—especially to the visitor who enters it for the first time—is spacious, delicate West Walton (62, 68, 73, 79) with its cluster-columns, wide expanses, and fine vaulting; or the cool, clean articulation of Whitechurch Canonicorum (72, 196). The transition from the Norman is perhaps best seen at New Shoreham (51, 53, 59), or at Faringdon or Blewbury crossings (61 and 86); or at Stoke-sub-Hamdon (75), where Norman nave and chancel are tucked within Transitional and Early English transepts, with a bewildering variety of windows, corbels, doors, etc., all round the church. Stanton Harcourt (83, 114, 146) is the genuine and integrated result on a small scale. Here, in the Early English period of the thirteenth century, the massive Norman and Saxon towers first gave way to soaring spires—as at Polebrook (81), Market Harborough (108), and Ketton (80) where much of the former Norman work was re-used (especially in the west front). Ottery St. Mary (77) is remarkable; it is an Early English copy of the Norman transeptal towers of Exeter cathedral, and provides, incidentally, a rare example of tasteful Victorian restoration (by Butterfield).

The Decorated style follows gradually upon Early English—built up from precedent to precedent. There is no mistaking the great strides forward in architectural skill and decoration, just as there is no mistaking the growth of trade, commerce and general prosperity after the Black Death had raised the status of labouring men, commerce had swollen the towns, and both influences had unleashed an agrarian and commercial revolution. Lethaby set the mid-point of Gothic at 1350. The Black Death was in 1348. By the end of the fourteenth century the English Perpendicular style was launched. The steady progress from Norman in 1150 to Perpendicular in 1400 mirrors the process—in parish, Parliament, town and manor, army and church—by which the Norman overlords were weaned to Englishry, and the nation as Chaucer knew it came to consciousness of itself, with English upon its lips.

It is almost *de rigueur* to eulogize the English parish churches of the late Decorated and Perpendicular styles—those portrayed in Plates 87 to 174. They are noble in conception and execution. They are as good in the small parish as they are in the prospering new towns; at Salle (88), Bramfield (102, 106; 199), or East Hagbourne (87), as at Pickering (118), Winchelsea (109) or Bampton (89), all of them late Decorated or early Perpendicular. The "wool churches" of

Marshland Norfolk (47, 153, 154) or Cullompton (124, 129, 141), or Thaxted (126) are as fine as those in the attendant seaports like Boston (160), or in north-country towns like Tickhill (148) and Thirsk (132); or in later Cornish towns and churches like Launceston (162); or in Devon villages like Stoke-by-Hartland (164).

Yet their beautiful clerestories and carved timber roofs, their rich tombs and fonts, lecterns and screens, their poppyheads and bench-ends, porches and towers—these also breathe the ambivalent vainglory and terror, combined, of *nouveaux riches* with uneasy consciences, the breaking-down of the earlier unity between Church and State, the consecrating of "great possessions" in this world in the hope of obtaining something in exchange for them in the world to come, and the almost desperate ostentation wherewith both rich and poor tried to convince themselves that their piety was as profound and all-pervasive as it had been for their Norman or Saxon forefathers. The plain truth is that what the churches were gaining in secular beauty, the Church was losing in spiritual values. It was the prelude to the Great Schism from which Europe and the world still suffers. And it was not confined to England.

There they still stand, splendid memorials of a splendid era in English history, with all their local variations of plan or elevation: greater width than length at Abingdon (149), walls almost all windows at Salisbury (175), blatantly battlemented as at Bromham (142), thrusting out chapels with the ships and trade-marks of their benefactors graven upon their walls, as at Tiverton and Cullompton (129, 141), and filled with tombs as remarkable as any in Christian Europe (105, 139, 189). Yet it is often in the smaller village churches of this period that the visitor will feel the steady pulse of England beating; as at Launcells (156), Torbryan (158, 182), Heckingham (186), and Baulking (93). The new centres of commerce have come up too fast, like their rich citizens. Their new big churches will remain, when their towns—like Cley, Blythburgh, Worstead (which gave its name to cloth), Southwold, Martock, Thaxted, Saffron Walden, and many another—have dwindled, leaving a mighty nave above a meagre congregation, and a terrible economic problem in our own day for priest and parishioners alike.

The landlords enclosed arable fields as grazing for sheep which provided the wool, thus denying land to the villagers; so villages vanished—as Wharram Percy vanished (183, 185)—leaving little churches unpeopled, and only a solitary house or farm. But then, as if in revenge, the rich trade with the Low Countries and Europe by way of East Anglia was wrenched away to the West. The Atlantic was opened in the sixteenth century. From that time on the great Perpendicular style gives way to Tudor, with its brick or fan-tracery and its rich, heavy porches.

The Perpendicular period gave us our finest craftsmanship in fonts and screens (105, 106, 137, and 138); in roofs, towers and tombs (120, 121, 122, and 189). But in impressing and im-posing itself on one, it loses personal intimacy and individuality. This sense of intimacy was to some extent brought back in ritual, as a by-product of both preaching and printing, after the Reformation. Henry VIII was logical, according to his lights, in preferring to see the royal arms where a rood-screen had been. But an even greater change was made after the long religious disputes of the Tudor period. The short Jacobean and Stuart period—interrupted as it was by the most violent outbreak of popular religious intolerance in English history, and the Civil War, —had, in fact, epitomized all the bewildering changes and variations of the century between the Reformation and the Restoration. And when Charles II came into his own again, there was

15

already a strong, middle-of-the-road, all-English movement for a reasonable compromise—in doctrine, style, ritual and architecture. The very sound of these words indicates what was coming: the Age of Reason.

The reader will see—in Plates 190 to 206—the steady development from the ornate but obvious Renaissance style known in England as Jacobean, to the classic and restrained Georgian style, shedding most of the Gothic (but never all) on the way. Preaching brings pulpits and box-pews. The chancel is opened up to the congregation in the nave. Screens have gone, and altar-rails have come. The one-chamber-church comes back as early as in Tudor times at East Guldeford (178) and two hundred years later at Cherry Willingham (217); elsewhere, later still. The rich men now build—as at Compton Wyniates after the destruction of the Civil War (191)—decently and reasonably, within their own properties again, and for the village as a whole (202 and 211). The Classical style—imbued with Gothic, as at Warwick (189, 197, 198), or in its pure English form which Wren did most to create, as at Ingestre (202, 203), or in the more antique Tuscan version of Mereworth (207, 210), or the brick and stone of Knutsford (220)— accords well with the Whig Revolution, the Bank of England, the first joint-stock-companies, and the most prosperous and reasonably carefree life the common people of England have ever known.

It was the last of the old England—on the eve of empire and Industrial Revolution, and of the first all-European war which was to last a whole generation. Yet even before the Napoleonic wars, and before these great changes occurred, the so-called "Gothic revival" was working its way into evidence: "so-called", because the building of Gothic churches in England, in one form or another, had in fact never ceased from the twelfth century onwards. We have mentioned Warwick, c. 1704; Shobdon (216), that priceless and fantastical example of "rococo Gothic", is of the mid-eighteenth-century; Hartlebury (225), by Rickman, is the genuine "Gothic Revival" article. It stands out among so many poor Victorian copies of greater masters' works because Rickman did not merely copy; he still ventured, with new materials and new ideas.

It is at this point that we decided to end our pictures. The suburbs of most English towns and cities are Victorian or later. They are filled with correct, plagiaristic modern versions of every "Gothic" style of English church, from Early English to Tudor. (There is, oddly enough, little inclination to copy the Classical styles; why, we cannot tell, but it is certainly not because of any difficulty of construction or material.) In the middle of these modern industrial cities, distended as they have become, are engulfed little village churches, like Benedict Biscop's Saxon tower-nave and church, nearly 1,300 years old, among the shipyards at Monkwearmouth. Another is the old parish church of Middleton (147), built-in by nineteenth-century industrialism, surrounded by Lancashire's smoking "pine-forest" of chimneys, but bravely wearing its wooden tower from an earlier age when out of the neighbouring forests also came the bows and arrows that won the Battle of Flodden Field. In this church, in 1524, Sir Richard Assheton —who was knighted for his gallantry on that field—placed a window to commemorate, by their names and likenesses, his company of Middleton archers. Not many Englishmen today notice that window, among the blackened streets of industrialism. Not many see the testimony of a parish church to the continuity of England and Englishmen.

The changing life of the country and its folk is reflected also in the cult of the Church of England. That has been implied by many things already mentioned. In this country, cult and ritual have varied perhaps more than in any other; and so have, correspondingly, the details of structure and decoration, of church furnishings and ornament.

We have seen that when churches first arose in England after two centuries of darkness, the chancel was the peculiar responsibility of the rector, the nave that of the community—whether the rector and community were ecclesiastics or laymen. From the earliest times of Christianity in Asia, there were bars or *cancelli* between the "chancel" and the nave. This division—sometimes of triple brick arches, as we saw—developed into what came to be called a screen: first of stone, later of painted wood, against which stood subsidiary altars, and on which was raised the rood with its loft. This kind of screen disappeared almost completely in the century of intolerant destruction between the Reformation and the Restoration, 1540 to 1660. But some such screens still remain, of breath-taking beauty even in their aged and neglected state (106 and 114).

Nor are these screens the only relics of the pre-Reformation Church when the life of Englishmen was so much more at one with that of their European neighbours. There are the hagioscopes or squints pierced obliquely through transeptal and other walls to give side-worshippers a view—and a sound, when much mumbling went on behind big screens—of the mysteries of the Mass (61). There are Sanctus bellcotes (163), mass-dials in the walls (39), piscinae and sedilia with or without canopies (83), and "leper windows" the purpose of which is still not definitely established (95). The side-altars—by the screens, at aisle-ends, or in porches—show the degrees alike of everyday devotion, and of ostentation. So do the tombs and epitaphs of the well-to-do who could lie in nave, aisle, or transept, in their "lairstalls" and under their "lair-stones"; the wall-paintings; the secular—often indelicate—carvings in the people's parts of the church; and the extraordinary wealth of gold, silver, jewels and precious stuffs belonging to the particular church (and the Church in general) for use in the chancel.

The Reformation took a century and a half to work itself out in England: from its Continental beginnings about 1500 to the Restoration of the Stuarts in 1660. Printing and preaching were its heralds. Under Elizabeth preaching became popular; the Bible was available in the common tongue; exposition of it was to open new fields of faith and conflict. Lecterns and pulpits now multiply—just as the screens, squints, carvings, and paintings had formerly been multiplied to inculcate forms and ceremonies. Morning and evening prayer was now often read within the nave alone. The new communion tables were also often located there, or placed lengthwise in the middle of the choir or chancel.

By the "time of troubles" in Charles I's reign the practices of the reformed Church of England had obviously led to widespread secularization of the holy places and their contents— school was often held in naves or even in chancels, and church and secular accounts were kept on communion tables. Archbishop Laud's attempt to resanctify church and cult—by allowing the "altar" to revert to the east end, enclosing it within "rails", and causing it to keep its place during communion—was soon overthrown by the Puritan Revolution, the Civil War, and the iconoclasm and vandalism of the fanatical Cromwellians and their far more extreme followers. Yet it was to Laud's systematization, in the main, that the Restoration reverted after 1660; so the established Church of England—unlike the "reformed churches" of Protestant Europe and

17

Scotland, but like most *secular* English institutions—contrived to conserve and to continue, with the minimum of revolution and the maximum of reform. The chancels—so long the bone of contention and the bane of Puritans—remained. So did the screens or "bars", though without "images" on them. Matins and evensong were now held in the nave, with the priest at the east end of it; the chancel, however, was open to all communicants—inside the *cancelli* or barriers— up to the altar, or communion table, which in general remained fixed at the east end of the sanctuary. All the other pre-Reformation chantries, side-chapels, transepts, aisles, etc., fell out of use, became pews, mortuaries, and so forth, or otherwise merged into the church proper.

Churches built after the Civil War embodied most of these changes: for example, they generally had no chancel behind a screen, but rather a nave and a sanctuary opening directly from it—almost indistinguishable, one from the other—as in the pure Classical style, which was itself indirectly derived from the earliest basilican plans (206). The population of England, how-ever, had now grown, slowly from the Reformation to the eighteenth century, and then rapidly between the ends of the eighteenth and nineteenth centuries. So the progression through the Classical period, and after, brought galleries along the sides and at west ends of churches— which led to great, and mainly unsolved, structural and stylistic difficulties (as at Blandford Forum, 218, and Rickman's Gothic Revival church at Hartlebury, 225).

One sometimes thinks of the Victorians as "restorers" out of existence of many beautiful churches and their contents. But they loved the English parish church; and they conserved much which their predecessors simply destroyed or allowed to fall into ruins. Their errors (as we deem them) arose from excess of zeal. The "Gothic Revival" had begun a century before the Victorians' version of it. Yet, although their worship of 14C Decorated or Early Perpendicular resulted in "mass-production suburban Gothic", it also initiated the ecclesiological movement of the 1840's and 1850's, with which came the religious and ritualistic revival. It was a return to Gothic and even pre-Gothic mystery and ritual, from the Classical rationality of the 1660–1760 period. It was perhaps, in a way, the first manifestation of the contemporary "flight from reason". So the priest returned to the chancel for both morning and evening prayer; both parts of Victorian churches came into constant use; and communicants once more began coming up merely "to the altar rails".

At that point our pictures cease. During the past hundred years—in the structure, furnishing and ritual of the English parish church—the developments, disputes and discussions have largely been about "old, unhappy far-off things, and battles long ago". There have been no really new schisms. And there have been no really new styles.

*

A word is due about the way this book was planned and made. It is, in the first place, intended as a companion volume to Dr. Martin Hürlimann's *English Cathedrals* and Dr. Hürlimann's and M. Jean Bony's *French Cathedrals*. But there are fewer than fifty properly designated cathedrals of the Church of England in the country, all told, and in a volume with roughly the same number of pictures Dr. Hürlimann dealt with seventeen of them. Ours has been a far more difficult task, first of selection, and secondly of compression; for the latest statistics tell us that there are in England alone over 12,500 parish churches; they range in date from the year 670 to our own day; they afford, therefore, more regional, stylistic and other variations than England's cathedrals, which were all built in four centuries, instead of thirteen.

First, then, as to our method of selection: we took the total of England's parish churches by counties, and reduced this to six broad regions. Significantly, though we had not so intended it, these six regions came very close to six of the early Saxon kingdoms. This enabled us to "weight" our national sample by the total number of parish churches occurring in each of these six regions, and then to see that most styles and periods were represented in each region. Thus, there are more people and more parish churches in modern "Southumbria" than in modern "Northumbria". The reasons date back to the paucity of settlements and roads in both Saxon and Roman times in the north, to the Vikings' devastations, and to William the Conqueror's laying waste of the north. Indeed, the bulk of the English people and their churches are still south of the river Humber. So more churches from the south are represented in this book. The same applies to particular regions, such as populous "Mercia" or "East Anglia"—"populous" in the sense of frequency of parishes and their churches.

So much for the quantitative aspect: the qualitative aspect presented still more of a problem. Dr. Cox (see Bibliography) was depreciatory of the quality of parish churches in "the northern six counties" (our "Northumbria"), where he said there were very few that could compare with those down south. In strict terms of aesthetic—whether of structure or contents—that is true. Yet it is only half the story; for Northumbria, "the North Country", has exercised a potent influence out of proportion to its population, parishes or property, on the arts, the faith of the Church of England, our social and political institutions (including that of the monarchy itself) and our trade, commerce and industry. So is it, at the other extreme, with Devon and Cornwall. We therefore tried to "weight" our sample of 159 parish churches—a sample of about one per cent of the grand total—for what most authorities agree is "quality" as well as for "quantity".

We encountered unforeseen difficulties, about which it is as well to be frank. Take, for example, the immensely important historical division between country and city: it has been easy to show here what a former England's social division in this respect achieved in its rural and urban churches; but it would have been impossible to deal fairly with the Victorian urban and suburban parish churches. The population of England alone when Victoria came to the throne was some 15 millions; when she died it had just about doubled; and, despite heavy emigration meanwhile, more even than this increase—a lot more, because of depopulation of the countryside—accrued to the cities, blowing them out into suburbs with row-or-terrace houses, and every kind of Gothic Revival parish church alongside every kind of Romanesque Revival Nonconformist church or chapel. Yet throughout the vast Victorian epoch, and to within living memory, "quantity" seems to carry the day over "quality". If we had stoutly maintained an accuracy of mere statistical "weighting", we fear we should have been unfair in the resulting portrayal of the English parish church through its thirteen centuries of life.

Then there is another problem of selection: a few churches we badly wanted to include could not be photographed. An enemy had destroyed them; or they were in process of repair from war-damage; or they were for purposes of normal maintenance clothed in fine steel scaffolding within or without; or war-damage to their surroundings rendered such photographs as we took unsatisfying or misleading. Such was our experience in many big cities—London in this respect was sadly *a per se*, but Bristol, Norwich, Plymouth, Coventry, Leicester, Liverpool, Manchester, Southampton, Lydd, and Taunton foiled our plans for one or other of the reasons mentioned.

Last among the problems we perforce had to solve—after our fashion—was the vexed one of strict terminology: what definition must we take of a parish church? It is a tougher nut to crack than it seems, for in thirteen centuries of uninterrupted life some churches began as cathedrals or minsters or collegiate churches and ended as true parish churches (Brixworth, Stow, Dorchester Abbey); some began as parish churches and ended as cathedrals (Bury St. Edmunds); some were both the one and the other through the ages (Sherborne); some were parish churches and are now but chapels-at-ease or not strict parish churches at all (Bradford-on-Avon, St. Laurence); some were cathedrals and are now but chapels (St. Peter ad Vincula, Bradwell-juxta-Mare, Essex); some were private chapels and are now parish churches (Compton Wyniates) and some (Wharram Percy) remain parish churches, but minus parish, priest, and congregation. We show examples of all these, and have solved the problem—to our own satisfaction—by making the least compromises; though we have admitted a chapel or two to show structural or other details, we have tried to confine ourselves to what can strictly be defined today as a parish church.

This record could never have been compiled without the closest collaboration between photographer and author, who are both zealous ecclesiologists. Together we visited 99 per cent of the churches here represented; shared the planning and selection both of churches and views; shared the noting and checking of details. For practical reasons, we have had to restrict the number of photographs reproduced to one-third of those taken, which naturally covered a greater number of churches.

Should our work result in furthering the proposal to record photographically much more —indeed, before it is too late, the whole—of the wealth and beauty manifested in England's parish churches, we should, for that reason alone, regard it as having been worth doing.

A last word: this book has been a labour of love, in which the friendship between its authors played no little part. Only those who have had to struggle, professionally, with the English climate—which is so much a part of our temperament as a nation—will know something of the anxieties and the disappointments we encountered. To illustrate the finest points of a church, inside and out, we have waited not merely for hours but for days and months—in some cases years; sometimes we have had to return in due season to a locality that had earlier stubbornly refused to provide the desired conditions. Lest this should deter any of our readers from visiting England's parish churches, let him or her also remember Baldwin Brown's apt phrase: "there is a special attractiveness in *the simple structure that has grown by a sort of happy accident into beauty*; and it is worth while inquiring how this comes about". We can testify that the most fruitful way of inquiring is to let the beauty of the churches, inside and out, grow upon one "by a sort of happy accident". The tale of beauty, the voices of stones, and the talk of the past can only be heard by those who take pains and patience. When heard, they are unforgettable.

In the hope that our experience will be shared—in the parish churches of England them/selves, or vicariously in these pages—this book has been planned and executed. But it could not have been made at all without the kindness of others, among whom we can only name here the Precentor of Norwich Cathedral (the Rev. A. G. G. Thurlow, M.A., F.S.A.), the Rev. Wynter Blathwayt, Mr. and Mrs. Clinton F. Chance, Miss Jane Munns, Miss Olive Cook, Miss Daphne Sparrow, and our sympathetic and painstaking publishers. To a host of helpful and hospitable incumbents who kindly eased our work we here return thanks; they are remembered by us, and in no small measure this book is also theirs. Last—but not least—we record gratitude to many lay folk in city streets and rural lanes, who gave us aid with parochial pride: folk tending the graves of a household, gravediggers and gardeners, garnishers of the House of God, boys who bicycled for keys, and girls from Sunday School who carried our messages or gear. In a measure this is their book too—as it is of all those throughout the world who can say, "Lord, I have loved the habitation of Thy house".

BIBLIOGRAPHICAL NOTE

ON English parish churches in general there is a wealth of good books, among which (for ordinary purposes, and apart from adequate illustrations of detail) may be mentioned *The Parish Churches of England*, by J. Charles Cox, ed., with additional matter, by C. B. Ford (Batsford, 1935) and *Parish Church Architecture*, by E. Tyrrell-Green (Society for Promoting Christian Knowledge, 1924). County by county there are the monumental detailed works of *The Victoria County History* and *The Royal Commission on Historical Monuments* where available, and for everyday purposes *The Little Guides* or *Murray's Guides*. The useful Shell Guides of pre-war days are being resumed, with their sections on the churches of each county; and many publishers after the war put out county books which are of service. Among these should especially be noted the new Murray's *Architectural Guides* under the admirable care of MM. John Betjeman and John Piper, and the new Penguin *Buildings of England* series under the editorship of Professor Nikolaus Pevsner. In both of these sets of books the notes on the churches are models of succinct counsel. Still on the general plane, of inestimable use and information for serious students, though ill-served with illustrations, is Miss M. D. Anderson's (Mrs. Trenchard Cox's) *Looking for History in British Churches* (Murray, 1951); and for beginners there is a useful little pocket-sized book by W. H. Riley, *English Church Architecture, 680 A.D.-1547 A.D.* (Hutchinson).

The antiquarian-minded should not omit to consult the Brandon brothers' *Parish Churches* (Bell, 1848) with their wonderful uniform-scale ground-plans and drawings; Rickman's genial pioneer work, *Gothic Architecture* (the sixth edition ed. and publ. by Parker is the best, since it conserves Rickman's Anglo-Saxon section in its proper setting); the volumes of *The Ecclesiastical and Architectural Topography of England* (Parker), Parker's own *Gothic Architecture* and *Glossary*, and the *Proceedings* of the Archaeological Institute (for counties and cities). For the churches of the City of London, antiquarians will consult the two volumes of 1838 (publ. by Tilt), *The Churches of London*, by Godwin and Britton, so meticulously drawn by Billings and engraved by Le Keux. Finally, for those both antiquarian- and meticulous-minded, there are the full files of *The Builder* and *The Ecclesiologist*, which testify to the great revival of concern for our national heritage of churches in Victorian times. Their analytical descriptions of structures can seldom be bettered. So much for the general field.

In the particular, no one can begin to appreciate our first ecclesiastical structures and arts without looking into the monumental volumes of Baldwin Brown's *Arts in Early England* (Murray); he is the giant in this landscape. Few seem to know so well his early *From Schola to Cathedral* (Edinburgh, David Douglas, 1886) with its provocative theory of the derivation of the first church-plans. Of uniform authoritativeness in their spheres are the late Sir Alfred Clapham's two volumes (Oxford) on *English Romanesque Architecture* (1930 and 1934), and Sir Thomas Kendrick's *Anglo-Saxon Art* and *Late Saxon and Viking Art* (Methuen, 1938 and 1949); while without Sir F. M. Stenton's classic *Anglo-Saxon England* (Oxford, 2nd ed., 1947) the student of our national beginnings would merely stumble. Clapham's *Romanesque Architecture in Western Europe* (Oxford, 1936) is a very useful handbook for travellers who want to understand more of the interrelationships of styles and structures in the darker ages of

Western Europe, and it has the merit of setting England's churches in that framework. Of the erudite works of such Continental scholars as Strzygowski, Puigh i Cadafalch, Rivoira and Hauck one can only make mention here—the work of illuminating England's and Europe's Dark Ages goes on apace—but modern Anglo-Saxons owe much to Lethaby's *Medieval Art* (Nelson, new edn., 1949) and to its editor and reviser, Professor D. Talbot Rice; G. G. Coulton's *Art and the Reformation*, etc.; and to Lethaby's little *Architecture* in the Home University Library (first publ. 1911) which is still as much of a provocative classic—after its fashion—as Sir Banister Fletcher's renowned and ponderous *History of Architecture*.

It is good that the Cambridge University Press has issued (1951) a new edition of A. H. Gardner's famous handbook, *English Medieval Sculpture*, without which many a parish church treasure would remain uncomprehended; and here one should mention also his *Alabaster Tombs* (Cambridge, 1940), Mrs. Katherine Esdaile's authoritative *English Church Monuments, 1510-1840* (Batsford, 1946), F. Bond's *Fonts and Font Covers* (Oxford, 1908) and *Wood-carvings in English Churches* (Oxford, 1911), C. J. P. Cave's *Roof Bosses in Medieval Churches* (Cambridge, 1948), J. Charles Cox's *English Church Fittings, Furniture and Accessories* (Batsford, 1923), F. H. Crossley's *English Church Monuments* (Batsford, 1921), M. D. Anderson's *Animal Carvings in British Churches* (Cambridge, 1938), F. J. Allen's *The Great Church Towers of England* (Cambridge, 1932), M. D. Whinney's *The Interrelation of the Fine Arts in England in the Early Middle Ages* (Benn, 1930), and Marcus Whiffen's *Stuart and Georgian Churches Outside London, 1603-1837* (Batsford, 1947-8).

Traversing all periods, styles and localities are A. Hamilton Thompson's *The Historical Growth of the English Parish Church* (Cambridge, 1911), Milburn's *Saints and their Emblems in English Churches* (Oxford, 1949), Englebert's *The Lives of the Saints* (Thames & Hudson, 1951) and—among so many good local productions—the outstanding books by C. J. W. Messent (*Parish Churches of Norwich & Norfolk*, 1936), H. Munro Cautley (*Suffolk Churches & Their Treasures*, 1938) and M. R. James (*Suffolk & Norfolk*, 1930).

Nearly every church visited by the authors contained (generally) reliable descriptions of structure and contents, either in purchasable booklet form or mounted on wooden hand-boards to be carried round by the visitor. Of some 350 churches we visited and photographed—and a further 100 or so which we visited but did not photograph—fewer than a dozen failed to offer this essential information.

Professor Sir F. M. Stenton's *Anglo-Saxon England* and Miss M. D. Anderson's *Looking for History in British Churches* provide exhaustive bibliographies of both books and articles; but we would specially mention three recent publications not therein quoted—*The Problem of England's Historic Churches*, the 11th Report of the Central Council for the Care of Churches, 1951 (Mowbray), containing valuable sections on all aspects of the problem and bibliographical references; two pioneering articles by MM. Eric G. M. Fletcher, M.P., and E. Dudley C. Jackson on Saxon "long and short work" and pilaster strips (*Journal of the British Archaeological Association*, third series, Vol. IX, 1944, and Vol. XII, 1949); and the stimulating lecture by Mr. M. W. Beresford of Leeds University to the Royal Geographical Society, published as "The Lost Villages of Medieval England" in *The Geographical Journal* of June 1951 (Vol. CXVII, Part 2), which gave us the rare experience of a visit to the village of Wharram Percy.

EVOLUTION OF CHURCH PLANS

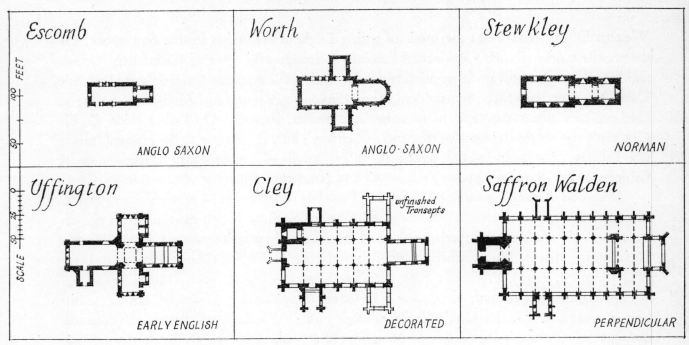

Escomb	Worth	Stewkley
ANGLO SAXON	ANGLO·SAXON	NORMAN

Uffington	Cley	Saffron Walden
EARLY ENGLISH	DECORATED	PERPENDICULAR

unfinished Transepts

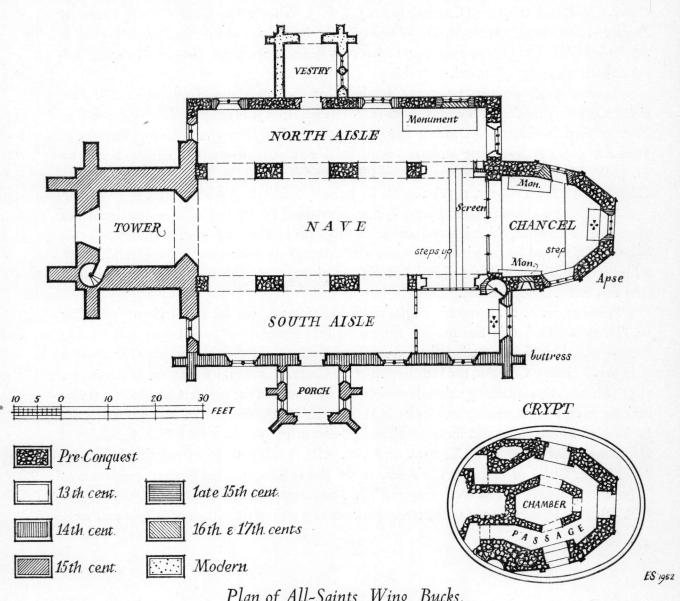

VESTRY

Monument

NORTH AISLE

TOWER   NAVE   Screen   CHANCEL   Mon.   step

steps up   Mon.   Apse

SOUTH AISLE

buttress

PORCH

CRYPT

CHAMBER

PASSAGE

ES 1952

Pre·Conquest

13th cent.   late 15th cent.

14th cent.   16th & 17th cents

15th cent.   Modern

Plan of All-Saints, Wing, Bucks.,
illustrating the growth of a Parish Church

NOTES

Certain abbreviations are used throughout the notes; these are: c. for about; St. for Saint; N, S, E and W for the points of the compass; 14C, etc., for 14th century, etc.; and EE, D and P for Early English, Decorated and Perpendicular respectively. Whenever there is more than one plate of the same church or its contents, the church and place are generally described in detail in the note accompanying the first of the plates. A glossary of technical terms appears on page 63.

1 ST. LAURENCE, BRADFORD-ON-AVON: view across nave from N porch to S porch. The date of this building is in dispute, but it is one of the earliest stone churches remaining and may have been one of Aldhelm's foundations (c. 700), later (c. 900–1000) re-roofed and decorated externally with the Carolingian blind-arcading visible in 2. The interior stonework, as in the present view, is crude from ground-level and improves to good coursing high in the walls, where local ashlar was used. The church—now a chapel to the N of the 19C parish church across the road—is more typical of the N country "Celtic" churches (see 3) than of the S country basilican kind. There are two remarkable carved flying angels in stone (probably part of a rood) set high in the E gable of the nave over its entry into the (smaller and asymmetrical) chancel. Entry into the nave is solely from the two N and S porches at the W end. There is no W door. The N and S porches seem to have been big enough for use as chapels; their entries into the nave are not aligned with the doorways to the outside world. The (later) blind-arcading on the exterior seems to have been carved *in situ* and not completed all round the building. See 2.

2 ST. LAURENCE, BRADFORD-ON-AVON: view from S. The S porch disappeared centuries ago, leaving the outline of the gable here visible.

3 ST. JOHN THE EVANGELIST, ESCOMB: view from S. This dates from c. 700, and is one of the early remaining Northumbrian stone churches built by, or soon after the time of, Benedict Biscop (others remaining are those of Jarrow and Monkwearmouth). This church is of rough-coursed stone and rubble. It has a longer and narrower nave (though not higher), and smaller square-ended chancel, than Bradford-on-Avon (1 and 2). The doorways, however, have square heads and are rebated, and there are proper voussoirs to the chancel-arch. Baldwin Brown thought this arch was a re-erected Roman arch from the neighbouring military stations. The stones of arches and jambs at Escomb are "through", i.e. go solidly through their walls in one piece, as in Roman military work. Bede records that Benedict Biscop brought masons from Gaul to build his stone churches. The inordinately long and narrow nave, and even narrower short chancel at Escomb, seem to bear out the theory of its Gaulish origin.

4 ST. NICHOLAS, WORTH: view from S to N transept with chancel-arch to the right. It is probably an 11C church and—rare for that time—has a long E apse, which possibly dates from the 9C, when the rest of the church was wooden. It is properly cruciform, with the transepts (chapels) by the chancel-arch (as in this Plate), unlike Bradford-on-Avon where the porches are at the W end (1 and 2). But the transepts at Worth are not truly opposed, and there is no proper crossing—the nave simply continuing straight up to the chancel-arch. The latter runs almost to the full width of the chancel; it is a noble work with proper voussoirs; and these also appear in the splendid transept arches. Masons' work, to receive plaster, is clearly visible. The attached shaft and rudimentary cushion-capital, carrying the chancel-arch, are noteworthy. There are two fonts in one, the lower probably Saxon, the upper EE. The pulpit, shown here, was brought from Worth in Germany and is dated 1557. See 20.

5 ST. MARY, BREAMORE: view into S porticus from base of tower. The church was built c. 1000; is of flint and rubble, formerly plastered, with stone quoins; and differs from Worth (4 and 20) in having a central tower, originally (as now) of wood on a flint-and-stone base. To N and S were two porticus. That to the N has

disappeared. This arch into the S porticus shows a rare and early use of cable-moulding along the edges of the massive impost on the W of the arch. The wall here is 3 ft. thick; the voussoirs are "through" stones; and round the voussoirs runs the only remaining stone-carved text in Anglo-Saxon—"HER SWUTELATH SEO GECWYDRAEDNES THE"—"Here is the Word (or Covenant) made manifest to thee (or which . . .)", apparently a reference to *Titus*, i, 3. Another stone in the wall conserves the letters "DES", so perhaps the two porticus arches and the chancel-arch bore continuous inscriptions relating to the ritual of the Mass. It is thought that transepts originated from such rudimentary porticus. There are the sad and mutilated remains of a Saxon rood—with a background of a captivating landscape—on the outer wall, within the 12C S porch at the W end; no less than seven Saxon windows; some fine "long-and-short" work and pilaster-strips; a "low side-window" or "leper-window" to the W of the N wall; and a good 14C E window. Breamore shows as well as any Saxon church the gap between the faces of the quoins and the present flint-walling, a gap that was originally taken up by plaster.

6 ST. BOTOLPH, HADSTOCK: view from nave through N door. This cruciform church is possibly Canute's minster, consecrated in his presence in 1020 to commemorate his victory over Edmund Ironside at "Assandun" (Ashdon is the name of the parish adjoining on the SE). The N door, restored, is partly Danish; it formerly bore a piece of the skin of a "sacrilegious Dane", now in the Saffron Walden museum; but though it is human skin, it may have been that of any common criminal, as flaying was then a common punishment for theft, etc. The door is set in a beautiful arch with carved and moulded imposts of Scandinavian inspiration, shown in the palmette motif. The nave and N transept of the church are original. A W tower and a N porch were added in the 15C. There is a massive square Norman font. See 113.

7 ST. JOHN THE BAPTIST, TUNSTALL: Roman votive stone "to Aesculapius and Hygiea" built into W wall of window on N side of nave. The stone lies on its side *in situ*. It comes probably from a nearby Roman military station. The church was dedicated to St. Michael until 1620. It is a fine, massive, fortress-like stone

structure of the 15C, admirably fitting into the bold contours of N Lancashire. There are some remains of 13C stonework (the original church). There is no division between chancel and nave; the S chancel aisle seems to be of the 16C; there was substantial restoration in 1847; and in 1907 all plaster was stripped from the inner walls. See 103.

8 ST. JOHN or ST. STEPHEN, KIRKBY STEPHEN: the "bound devil" of the remnant of Jellinge-style cross-shaft at the W end of the nave. It may be the false god, Loki, bound and awaiting judgment. This late Scandinavian, flat, strapwork-like, shallow sculpture, of more barbaric inspiration than earlier styles, is naturally most frequently found all over the N, where the 10C and 11C Viking and Norse raiders and settlers penetrated (see 10 and 13). Kendrick (*Late Saxon & Viking Art*, Methuen, 1949, p. 90) compares this design with the Crucifixion on Harald Gormsson's monument. It was common to find heathen subjects incorporated in Christian crosses: Sigurd and the Bird, for example, appear at the base of the beautiful cross in Leeds parish church; and in the famous early "stave churches" (wooden) of Norway there are dragons to protect the building (see 36), while the "old gods" Odin, Thor, etc., are used as capitals of the pillars holding up the nave roof, grimacing about the task assigned to them.

9 ST. PETER, BRITFORD: carved stone panels, c. 800 but possibly earlier, in arch of portal to chamber N of nave. Less remains in a similar arch to the S; but over the S door the Saxon bricklayer has laid his voussoirs wrongly, with their thick ends pointing inwards. Kendrick (*Anglo-Saxon Art to 900 A.D.*, Methuen, 1938, p. 116 and pp. 180–1) calls attention to the similarity between the lobed arrangement of "fat leaves", inside the volutes of the Classical vine-pattern in the two long upright panels, and that on the fragments of the Reculver cross (one of our earliest Christian remains) in Canterbury crypt, and in Sant' Apollinare in Classe, Ravenna. The present cruciform church dates from c. 1280–1330, the central tower (and a square-ended chancel which covered the original E apse) being added c. 1325. The old (? Saxon) font "shaped like a lily" was given away to a church in Australia, c. 1873.

10 ST. PETER, HEYSHAM: base of cross in churchyard, c. 850, showing traditional Northumbrian scrollwork

on the narrow side, and Southern panel-patterning (part of a more ambitious design) on the wide face. Heysham had more Christian and heathen settlements than most places in England: first Irish (the Celtic church), then Anglian (Northumbrian), then Norse (by way of the Isle of Man), then Saxon again (the place-name means "Hessa's ham"). The existing EE nave leads to the square-ended chancel of c. 1350 (formerly an E apse); the chancel-arch, of massive size, and without moulding, springs direct from the walls, from imposts with cable-mouldings. There is also a famous Scandinavian "hog-back" stone in the churchyard. The S aisle is of c. 1250; the N aisle is modern.

11 ST. JOHN THE BAPTIST, INGLESHAM: the late Saxon (c. 1000–1050) Virgin and Child in the SE corner of the chapel at the E end of the S aisle. The shallow carving (1 to 2 in. deep) is typical of late Wessex sculpture, when the "Winchester" type of manuscript-decoration was copied in stone. Thus, this figure shows the "anguished stoop" of the Virgin and Child, also visible in MSS of the Winchester school. The *manus Dei* coming into the picture from the "frame" at the top right, is also an imitation of MS work. This church was William Morris's favourite, and he helped to restore it in 1888–9. It shows work from the 11C to the 19C. A 14C stone S porch with a niche in a noble gable leads through a Norman door into a Transitional-EE (c. 1200) S aisle with 15C windows. Chancel-arch and square-ended chancel are EE. Other contents include a fine two-decker early-17C pulpit; lovely box-pews of late-16C to 18C date (those in the choir being particularly fine late-17C); a charming 18C box-pew at the W end of the N aisle; a 15C barn-like trussed roof to nave, and an early 14C roof (boarded) to chancel with tie-beams; deep-splayed EE windows in the chancel over three Norman sedilia in the N wall; traces of murals round the altar (? 14C); late-14C or early-15C carved wooden screens joining the nave arcades; a pleasing Royal Arms of William IV (1830) over the centre of the arcade on the N; and many traces of gold and other colouring round the chancel, in the S porch piscina, etc. The church was underpinned in 1914, when it was found to be without any foundations. See 65 and 70.

12 ST. JOHN THE BAPTIST, BARNACK: the Christ Majesty at E end of N aisle. The date of this sculpture is disputed. Clapham thought it "late pre-Conquest"; Kendrick puts it after the Conquest, but as the work of a Saxon sculptor. There is still something of the manuscript influence about it, but also (especially in head and shoulders) of the Rhineland style of the 11C. The church itself is famous for its mid-10C Carolingian W tower with stone pilaster-strips and carved panels and other decorative motifs thereon. (The belfry over the tower is of later date.) The famous E arch of the tower into the nave (17) shows remarkable mouldings of a pure Saxon 10C type; and the exterior of the tower shows the Carolingian acanthus motif in carved panels. In three of the tower-windows the stone *transennae*, or lattices to keep out weather but let in light, survive. The nave arcades are Norman and Transitional, with EE aisles; the S arcade capitals are EE, those of the N arcade, Norman; there is a fine Norman arch to the N side of the old chancel; and there are good D sedilia and a piscina in the (extended) chancel, which is both Norman and D. The fine S porch has EE arcades; and there is an EE chantry on the S.

13 ST. ANDREW, MIDDLETON-BY-PICKERING: Saxon wheel-head crosses and remains in N aisle. This church is one of the richest in England in such remains. They are mostly of the Danish and Norse "time of troubles" (9C and 10C) and show, in their wheel-heads, shallow surface-carving and broad strap- or knot-work, Scandinavian influences; but the main designs, as Kendrick says, and the execution are in the old Celtic and Saxon tradition. The finest of the three—that standing back in the middle—shows most clearly the older Celtic-Saxon interlacings; the cross-head has a boss; the shape of the head indicates a slightly earlier date; and there is no separation of head from panel, the shaft-face-decoration running continuously into the decoration of the head. The W tower, up to the second stage, is Saxon; probably late 10C or 11C. The earliest Norman work here seems to be of c. 1130 when the nave was rebuilt and the N aisle opened; the S aisle was opened c. 1200, when the upper stage was added to the W tower and the chancel-arch rebuilt. Both nave aisles were rebuilt c. 1300, and in the 15C the clerestory was added, the N aisle having a stone bench running right round it up to the former E altar platform. Junction of Saxon, Norman and 13C work is visible on the outside N wall, on both sides of the tower. There are good EE and D doors N and S.

14 ALL SAINTS, BRIXWORTH: Clapham calls it "perhaps the most imposing architectural memorial of the 7C yet surviving N of the Alps". The view is from the S. The church was originally basilican with E apse, and crypt below; a W narthex and outer atrium; and a wide, two-aisled nave. It is thought to be the minster founded by the monks of Medeshamstede (later Peterborough), c. 670, and is built of stone, Roman brick and rubble. It is now reduced to the line of the original nave arcading. The original aisles, N and S portions of the narthex, and outer walls have disappeared (when the Danes destroyed so much in the 9C). The Plate shows the original Saxon aisle arcade on the S with the original clerestory above; but roof, S door, windows, battlement, the upper belfry over the old W tower, and the newel-staircase tower still farther to the W, are later additions. It can be seen in this Plate (and in 19) that the Roman brick arches of the original S aisle (which were then, of course, over openings, forming piers) are crudely built; they "spring" on the slant from their rudimentary imposts, and are not centred and turned radially as in Roman or Byzantine work of the period. There was originally—as in Reculver and the other first Roman-Kentish churches, and in Bradwell-juxta-Mare, Essex—a triple-arched brick screen between nave and presbytery, of which the springing can be seen on the N side by the present single chancel-arch. The crypt has disappeared, but not the ambulatory (originally covered in); there is a fine (? 7C) round-headed door from the presbytery into a N porticus (disappeared) which probably formed the E end of the now destroyed N aisle, as at Bradwell-juxta-Mare; but no trace remains of one on the S of the presbytery. In the troubles of the late 9C and 10C the semicircular newel-stair turret was added to the remaining central portion of the W narthex and tower. Giving into the nave on the E face of the tower is a (rare) three-light round-headed window with two baluster-shafts carrying imposts, and below this there are traces of other openings into the nave from the W tower. In the S doorway, inside and on the jamb, is a late Roman or Byzantine (? Syrian) carved stone eagle; but the stone is dowelled as though for a cross-shaft, and it may now be set on its side. Near the pulpit is the lower part of an Anglian (? Mercian) cross-shaft with typical 8C or 9C Anglian interlacing. There are some fine early Norman-French tomb-slabs in the floor of the presbytery; a 14C reliquary of St. Boniface near the pulpit; and a good 14C window in the chancel. It

thoroughly deserves Baldwin Brown's designation as "the most instructive monument in the early history of our national architecture". See 19.

15 ST. MATTHEW, LANGFORD: view from SW. This early 11C church shows many Carolingian features: the central (instead of W) tower, pilaster-strips with stepped head-blocks, the acanthus on the capitals of the tower-shafts, and two figures holding up the defaced sundial on the tower. The Saxon church probably had an E apse, true to Continental models with central towers. The present square-ended chancel is EE and D. The EE pinnacles at the W end give a bizarre effect (69). The church possesses two remarkable external stone Saxon roods: one, visible in this Plate, in the gable of the later S porch, and the other on the E wall of the same S porch. Of these, the latter—with its (rare) long drapery to wrists and ankles—is assigned to the 10C. The crossing, internally, and the chancel-arch and mouldings are all late Saxon work. See 69.

16 ST. MARY, SOMPTING: the only surviving example in England of the "Rhenish helm" or "Rhineland spire". It is on an early 11C W tower. Features of Rhenish Carolingian style are also the pilaster-strips on the tower walls, the two-light round-headed tower windows divided by baluster-shafts, and some windows with triangular-heads. (See 29 and 30.) The church is cruciform without aisles. Exceptionally, the N transept has an E aisle, and the S transept has a narrower E aisle with a recess similar to a rudimentary (? or remains of a) chapel on its E side. The N transept arcade is Transitional to EE; the E chapels in this transept show EE stone vaulting and lancets. The S transept shows earlier Norman work. The Saxon or early Norman font is in the little barrel-vaulted recess or chapel to the E. The most arresting work inside the church, however, is the stone carving: on the E arch of the W tower into the nave (see 29), in the N transept, and in the S transept (see 30), as well as in the nave itself. The Saxon church seems to have been mainly overlaid by a Norman building with central tower in the 12C.

17 ST. JOHN THE BAPTIST, BARNACK: view from N aisle towards the E arch of the W tower. Here the peculiar mouldings of the tower arch, noted by Clapham as "perhaps the most remarkable example of mouldings of the native (Saxon) type", are shown; "the result is

barbaric in the extreme, and does not seem to have inspired any copyist". The EE font is also shown here. It is engraved in Rickman's book. See 12.

18 ST. BENE'T, CAMBRIDGE: E arch and face of W tower from nave. This later Saxon arch (? late 10C) should be compared with that of Barnack, 17, from which it differs considerably, in the rare carvings at the springing of the arch, in the "filled-out" moulding of the responds, in the ribbon-like, fluted effect of the outer moulding all round the arch from ground-level, and in the excellent "long-and-short" work of the aces of the arch. The exterior of this W tower shows three stages; mid-wall baluster-shafts support a long through-stone abacus in the belfry windows; and the quoins of the tower protrude from the present wall-face, showing where the plaster surface once ran. The original Saxon church had neither aisles nor transepts and probably ended in an E apse; in the latter half of the 13C the old nave was rebuilt to the original dimensions, and aisles were thrown out. The chancel, now square-ended, has been raised; but the bases of the original chancel-arch are still visible. The church is noted for its parish clerk of c. 1650, Fabian Steadman, who invented change-ringing.

19 ALL SAINTS, BRIXWORTH: view from presbytery, looking W to E face of W tower. The crude springing of the re-used Roman brick arches of the nave piers is less clearly visible here than in 14; but the sharp eye will detect the odd, stilted springing of the present chancel-arch from the buttressed remains of the original triple-arched brick screen (right of pulpit). The various openings of the W tower into the nave are also shown here.

20 ST. NICHOLAS, WORTH: view from chancel, through chancel-arch, along N wall of nave and into N transept. Yet another style of moulding is shown in this chancel-arch, as compared with those in 17 and 18. The through-stone bases and abaci of the round-headed Saxon windows, their mid-wall turned baluster-shafts, and the stonework of these windows are best seen from this angle. See 4.

21 ALL SAINTS, EARLS BARTON: W tower, c. 935. This is the most strikingly ornate Carolingian edifice left in England. Most noteworthy are the five-light belfry windows with banded baluster-shafts and single-stone round-headed arches above; the Rhineland-Carolingian pilaster-strip patterning, reminiscent of primitive woodwork; the "long-and-short" work of the tower quoins, here showing very clearly the gap left by the missing plaster surface; the moulding of the arch in the W door; the triangular-headed little windows in the third stage; and the crosses over, and alongside, the flat-arched pair of windows on the S face of the tower. The late 11C Norman chancel remains, with fine arcades on each side and P windows above, and there is a late Norman door in the 15C S porch. The E arch of the tower into the nave is Transitional, set within the framework of the original Saxon "long-and-short" work.

22 ALL SAINTS, STAPLEHURST: decorative ironwork on 11C wooden door in S porch. Clapham describes this door (and its famous companion at Stillingfleet, Yorkshire) as 12C; but we think the iron Viking ships, serpents, fish, sun, moon, etc., are Scandinavian and of magical as well as Christian import; and as there was once a Saxon church on this site, it may be that the later Norman building—one with nave and chancel only, and a (rare) tower on the S side by the E bay of the nave—incorporated some Saxon remains, of which this door was one. On the outer face of the N wall are remains of herring-bone Norman stonework. The single S aisle is beautifully roofed (first half of 15C) with fine king-posts; the tower is of the same date, the inner arch into the nave having mouldings running straight up and over from ground-level, and a typical Kentish turret stairway. The rebuilt P chapel is separated from the D chancel by an EE arcade—quite an instructive juxtaposition of styles.

23 ALL SAINTS, WING: the late 10C apse and later church from the lych-gate. See also the ground-plan of this church on p. 24, where we use it to illustrate the growth of a parish church. The (rare) seven-sided apse shows typical Rhineland-Carolingian pilaster-strips, blind arcading (first stage) once pierced with lights, and triangular-headed arcading (formerly pierced with lights) in the upper stage. The big chancel-arch is the largest Saxon arch left in England, and there is a Saxon window above it with mid-wall baluster-shaft. The nave arcades are also original, with their massive rectangular piers, up to the E arches which are EE. The S aisle was rebuilt in the 14C; S porch, W tower and roof

are of the later 15C; and at the E of the N aisle is the fine pure-Italian-Renaissance altar-tomb of Sir Robert Dormer, who died in 1552. There are many fine Dormer and other memorials, plaques and monuments, including a mural tablet in the nave to the memory of Henry Fynes, said (by Cole) to have been "done by Roubiliac". The rood-screen and S aisle-screen are good examples of early 16C work; and the font is 15C.

24 HOLY TRINITY, COLCHESTER: triangular-headed portal of re-used Roman brick at base of W tower. Note the bricklaying of the triangular arch, which has scarcely progressed (save in the patterning) since the 7C (cf. Brixworth, 14 and 19). Roman bricks, especially in E Anglia, were often re-used; here, even the tower quoins are made of them. The E wall of the tower into the nave is older (probably early 10C), as the 11C tower is an addition. The chancel was rebuilt in the mid-14C; the S arcade and S aisle were added a little later; and the S chapel and its arcade built—or rebuilt—in the late 15C.

25 ST. ANDREW, BISHOPSTONE: typical tall Saxon S porch, with 12C Norman four-stage W tower. Baldwin Brown thought the Saxon nave and S porch were 8C or 9C, probably because of the megalithic quoins (seen here), but this seems too early; by the flint and rubble work of the walls, and the slight outer splay and deep inner splay of the windows, it would seem more likely that they were late 9C or early 10C. The porch was a chapel; its rebuilt outer portal is set centrally while the inner one into the nave is set against the W wall, thus allowing for the inclusion of an altar to the E. The outer doorway is 12C Norman, but over the gable can be seen a Saxon sundial bearing the name "EADRIC" above the dowel-hole. The W tower, N aisle (only), and choir were added in the 12C; and the fine chancel (square-ended) between 1180 and 1200. The Saxon walls are characteristically higher and thinner than the later Norman walls—a feature which often surprises people who think of the Saxons as poor builders. The tower quoins are of Caen stone, Bishopstone being near the sea. On the S wall of the tower is a striking 12C carved tomb-slab in local stone and of decidedly Eastern inspiration; birds drinking from an urn, an Agnus Dei, and a cross, all interlaced within a cable pattern. It is thought to be inspired by ivory work. Its motifs may have been brought back from the Crusades.

26 ST. MARY, CHICKNEY: Saxon chancel, nave and 14C W tower. It is a small, typical early church—W tower, aisleless nave and square-ended chancel—built of rubble, with some crude stone-coursing. The windows are double-splayed; the N and S walls of the nave were cut back at the E ends, forming arched recesses, in the 15C; the chancel-arch has been much changed at various dates (but remains typically narrow); and the chancel was extended and squared-off by right angles in the 13C. There is a good early 15C font; an old mensa of the original altar, rediscovered during the restoration of 1858; and a S porch, probably of the 15C. The ground-plan—on p. 105 of Clapham's first volume on pre-Conquest churches (see Bibliographical Note, p. 22)—looks like a schoolboy's first essay in planning; there is scarcely a right angle in this Saxon church.

27 ST. JAMES, AVEBURY: view across W end of nave from S porch. This picture gives a good impression of the progress of styles and periods in a parish church: the nearby portal, with its orders, is Norman; the deeply internally splayed roundels of the clerestory are Saxon; as are also the two round-headed windows pierced in the nave walls to the W of the EE bay. The stepped stonework round the nearer pier shows the thickness of the plaster surface. Wooden shutters, to keep out the weather, were inserted into the centres of the two Saxon windows, which are splayed both ways. The N and S aisles are 12C; there is a fine squint from the S aisle; and nave and aisle arches are 1811 Gothic Revival. The 14C chancel is bigger than the Saxon one; the W tower is 15C; and there is a fine font (45).

28 ST. MICHAEL, MELBOURNE: Norman 12C capitals S of crossing, E side. This carving shows the (? Burgundian or Central French) influence brought into English work by the Normans, particularly in the two capitals to the left; that farther to the right shows more of the native Saxon style. The massive interior is better seen in 46, where a fuller description is given.

29 ST. MARY, SOMPTING: the E arch of the W tower, from the nave. This is the carving mentioned in 16. There is —for all its oddity—a trace of the coming Norman style about this ambitious Saxon arch.

30 ST. MARY, SOMPTING: 12C carving in E wall of S transept. It shows a seated bishop, who is also a saint,

giving the benediction and either holding a book or taking holy water from a (?) stoup with his other hand. The framework is Transitional; the capitals of the columns have strange abaci superimposed on them; and the treatment of crozier, drapery and features bears a striking similarity to the "caricature" or exaggerated style of Norman carving (cf. size of hands and fingers, head, and shoulders) also found at Barfreystone (37) and elsewhere in S England and N France at this time.

31 ST. MARY, IFFLEY: the 12C W front. There are capitals to the shafts of the outer orders of the three arches in the upper stage, but none in the great W portal below, with its hood-mould of signs of the Zodiac (see Brookland, 43) and its superimposed orders of beak-heads and chevrons. The central round window has been restored. Nave, central tower and chancel formed the original church, which now consists of nave, choir (tower above), and a perfect EE chancel. The two tower arches (the one to the W was the original chancel-arch) are fine specimens; there are black marble shafts in the angles of the arches on the W; and the vaulting of the original chancel (now choir) is still there. There is an external Norman newel-stair turret to the tower on the N, and a very fine S door with even more ornate treatment than the other portals, windows and arches, including capitals showing knights in combat. There is also a doorway to a 15C rood-loft. Rickman (see Bibliographical Note) gives many engravings of the details of Iffley church as it was over a century ago, but in his seventh edition, p. 100, makes the serious error of confusing Ketton W end with that of Iffley, see 80. See also 34.

32 ST. MARGARET, HALES: view from SW. The church has a simple Norman W tower, of typical round coursed flint with rubble flushwork round the top, aisleless nave, and apsidal chancel. Nave and chancel are thatched. The W end of the nave is buttressed (visible here) and the articulation of the tower into this end of the nave suggests that the whole of the W end of the church is earlier, perhaps Saxon, at least in the lower stages. Below the W gallery are remains of the rood-screen still showing fine red and green colouring. There further remain some late 13C painted designs over the E window of the chancel; an early 14C painting in good condition in the E window of the S side of the nave; and a St. Christopher and Child of c. 1400

at the W end of this S wall, the Child having an early type of halo. See 35.

33 ST. MARY, STOW: from W. This is the "mother cathedral" of Lincoln, and much Saxon stonework of a high order remains, particularly at the crossing both within and without. The megalithic quoins indicate early Saxon work at the crossing and transept-ends, being large and rough and with no trace of "long-and short" work. They seem to confirm the account of the burning of the original church by the Danes at the end of the 9C. The chancel roof was probably stone-vaulted (here visible) some 50 years after the rest of the Norman work was done; and there is a notable miniature arcade in the chancel wall (visible here, by the altar). The font is EE; there is a splendid (but fast fading) painting of St. Thomas à Becket on the E wall of the N transept; and some good 15C bench-ends remain in the nave.

34 ST. MARY, IFFLEY: view from chancel through choir and base of tower, looking W. See 31. The nearer arch was the original chancel-arch and shows both the springing of the stone vaulting-rib and the lozenge-decoration on the face of the pier to the extreme right of picture.

35 ST. MARGARET, HALES: view from SE, showing apsidal chancel with its remains of the Norman course of windows (blocked), buttresses, and the queer articulation of round W tower into the square W end of the nave. See 32.

36 STS. MARY AND DAVID, KILPECK: gable and corbel-table of W front. The stone-carving, reminiscent of Scandinavian metal-work, and the almost Aztec serpents' mouths, reminiscent of the dragons at the peaks and gables of wooden Scandinavian buildings, compare oddly with the more Franco-Norman florid carving of the corbels and shaft-capitals (see 40). The NE angle of the nave probably dates back as far as the 9C, but this simple aisleless, towerless nave and apsidal stone-vaulted chancel were built c. 1110. It was restored and rebuilt c. 1150-75, and well restored in 1864 and 1898. The bold massive moulding of the chancel-arch, and the freakish carvings of superimposed and disproportioned human figures there (? one of St. Peter with a key on his shoulder), are features impossible to match elsewhere in England (see p. 13 of Introduction).

There is a Norman font of unusual design and work-manship; a 12C stoup on the N side of the chancel-arch, with two arms encircling it and four serpents on its base; and a 17C oak W gallery. There is remarkable stone carving throughout this church, both internally and externally; and the carvings of the corbel-table on the S side of the apse outside feature the indelicate *Sheila-na-Gig* or "woman of the castle", which is ex-tremely rare on the chancel of a church, and may have had some connection with the adjoining castle to which the church belonged.

37 ST. NICHOLAS, BARFREYSTONE (ALSO BARFRESTON): the E end and wheel-window, strikingly French in style. Though Franco-Norman in so many ways, the church is simply an aisleless, towerless nave and square-ended chancel, with a comparatively rare triple chancel-arch of which the two side-arches are blocked. The chancel has two single-splay Norman windows aside and the (rare) Franco-Norman wheel-window in the gable end of the E end; the other E windows are lancets set between the arcading. There are richly carved winged beasts round this wheel-window, and inset carved figures in niches and roundels N and S of it (here visible). The corbel-table, seen both here and in 38, runs all round; it is one of the finest left in England. It will be seen in 38 that the nave-arcading has Transi-tional arches while the chancel has Norman arches to its arcading. The two arches over the S portal are asym-metrically placed. Inside, fine disproportionate and cari-cature-like carvings of animals are combined with many familiar and rare mouldings round heads of windows and doors, and below windows. An interesting string-course of Grecian type—with a "spotted ribbon" effect —runs round the lower course of the chancel, and was engraved by Rickman. On the inner faces of the capital on the E side of the S portal are Crusaders or jousting knights (see 39), and many *graffiti* Crusaders' and other crosses; and on either side of this portal there are many mass-dials. The church was originally built late in the 11C; then it was restored and overlaid with Caen stone (like many churches near the English seacoast in Norman times, when shipping stone was cheaper than bringing it overland from English quarries) c. 1180. The original Transitional chancel-paintings—necessarily de-stroyed in the restoration of 1840, which saved the church—were copied and are to be seen in the quarters of the Society of Antiquaries in London. See also 38, 39.

38 ST. NICHOLAS, BARFREYSTONE: view from S, showing the upper ashlar overlay in Caen stone and the lower rubble walls, mentioned in 37.

39 ST. NICHOLAS, BARFREYSTONE: S portal. Compare and contrast this with the S portal of Kilpeck facing it, and noted in 40; and see also 37 and 38 above. Cru-saders or jousting knights with lances can be seen on the capital of the inner shaft of the right-hand side of the portal; so can mass-dials on either outer face of the portal; and the rich Majestas Domini in the tympanum is set between figures of a lord and lady, perhaps Adam de Port and the Norman lady Mabil d'Orval whom he married in 1180. Scenes from the life of a Norman manor are shown in the outer order: 1 and 14 show soldiers; 2, starting from bottom left, the lady of the house; 3, the armourer; 4, the cellarer drawing ale or wine; 5, the viol-player; 6, the scribe; 7, the villein with flail or hoe; 8, the forester whose arrow has left the bow; 9, the carpenter adzing wood; 10, the miller with staff and sack; 11, 12 and 13 are said to represent Elijah, John the Baptist and David tearing a lion's jaws apart (? Samson); and 14, shows the soldier again. The adjacent semicircular moulding, inwards, shows recrea-tional subjects—music, love, dancing, etc.

40 STS. MARY AND DAVID, KILPECK: S portal; see also 39 immediately above, and 36. Each individual stone here is more symmetrically, severely and geometrically carved than are those of Barfreystone noted immediately above. The carving is probably copied from drawn wire-work or metal-work (see Clapham, Kendrick, and others cited in the Bibliographical Note on p. 22). The archstones of the portal (outermost order of the arch) are executed continuously, giving the effect of a neck-lace or wristlet. There is a trace of Saxon strap-work about the design in the (restored) tympanum.

41 ST. MARY, GREAT CANFIELD: capital of W shaft of S portal. This shows many traces of Danish work, and is often termed (wrongly, we think) Norman. The broken chevron pattern on the abacus, the (rare) line of swastikas on the top of the door-jamb to the right, and the geometrical shallow carving of the capital (a formal face and birds) all appear before the Norman period and are of the school represented at Had-stock, 6, Great Paxton and elsewhere in the Essex-Cambridgeshire-Huntingdonshire region. The famous

wall-painting on the splays of the E window, and in an arched Norman recess, is late 13C. There are some 13C lancets and a wooden porch and belfry of the 15C.

42 ST. GONAND OF THE ROCK, ROCHE: Transitional or EE font. This is often termed Norman, but shows, in the naturalism of the oblique-facing heads of the shafts, designs on the bowl, and bases of the shafts that it is of a later date, cf. Altarnun, 151. All styles—of structure, fonts and other church furniture—persisted longer in Cornwall than elsewhere.

43 ST. AUGUSTINE, BROOKLAND: Norman lead font. See also that of Dorchester, 71. This font has an upper course of the signs of the Zodiac (rare, but see Iffley, 31); and a lower course of the months and occupations associated with them, the names of the signs and months being placed above each panel. One can read "Leo, Virgo, Libra, Scorpio, Sagittarius" (though not exactly so spelled) along the upper course; and "Iuillet, Aust (?), Setembre, Vitovre (?) Novembre" along the lower. As there are 20 arches in each tier, zodiac and months are repeated. The church—whose remarkable detached wooden spire is seen and noted in 166—was built c. 1250. The N porch (entry) is 14C with good barge-boards, formerly closed by spiked shutter gates. The (13C) chancel has piscina and sedilia with early pointed arches and EE hood-mouldings and shafts, dating from c. 1250.

44 ST. PETER, NORTHAMPTON: Saxon slab (? cross-shaft) and Norman pier at E end of S aisle. The Saxon carving shows later Scandinavian influences, but retains the earlier interlaces and birds-in-a-vinescroll. The Norman capitals are of markedly Southern (? Central France or Burgundy) type, some pillars being banded half-way up by similar carvings. The church is remarkable in many ways: it never had a chancel-arch, but there was a rood-screen leading into the square-ended chancel. It has a fine W arch, spanning the nave where the W tower abuts; an arcade running the entire length of the church, with piers and columns of various kinds, all with elaborately carved capitals; a fine E end with three stages of round-headed windows; and an unusual W tower, with (rare) circular buttresses at its NW and SW angles. There is a (blocked) Norman clerestory running the length of the nave externally, now

appearing as blind-arcading, and above it a fine corbel-table with heads and grotesques. The W tower has proper blind-arcading, and on its W face at the second stage the original central W portal has been inserted (*minus* its other original orders).

45 ST. JAMES, AVEBURY: font. We take this to be late Saxon because of its un-Norman shape, upper course of foliated and interlaced pattern, and crude interlaced round-headed arches in the lower course, springing from columns with massive abaci. It may, however, be early Norman, executed by a Saxon craftsman to a Norman's instructions. See 27, and compare the foliated pattern of the upper course with that in the tympanum at Kilpeck in 40.

46 ST. MICHAEL, MELBOURNE: nave, clerestory, rood-screen with three lights, and crossing, from W. See also 28. The ambulatory in the original clerestory is shown; also the original corbels and wall-shafts—whence sprang the roof-trusses—together with the later ones. Clerestory arches are Norman on N, Transitional or EE on S.

47 ALL SAINTS, WALSOKEN: Norman arcades, P clerestory and roof, and Transitional chancel-arch, from W. The W tower has a double EE window in the second stage and a fine E arch into the nave. The roof is remarkable for its low pitch, massive carved trusses with figures (visible here along the walls) and winged angels. Outside, the W tower (EE base) and portal are very imposing. The church was built c. 1146, but widened c. 1320. There is a fine screen before the S chapel, with traces of colour and gilding; a remarkable (? early 15C) wall-painting on the E face of the tower-arch into the nave, of Solomon's judgment; and a noble octagonal Seven-Sacrament font (1544) for which see 137.

48 ST. MARY, PATRIXBOURNE: S portal beneath gable in central tower; a rare example of a Norman portal set in a slight built-out gable. The 12C flint and rubble nave and chancel remain, with an EE aisle to the S and a modern N aisle. The chancel has two single-splay windows aside and three at the E end, with a smaller wheel-window than that at nearby Barfreystone (37) over them. The S portal externally is more Anglo-Norman than that at Barfreystone; there is a Norman niche in the gable, which contains the indistinct figure

of a lamb with a (?) dove on its back. The fine wood-shingled broach-spire is probably D, on a Norman square tower.

49 HOLY SEPULCHRE, CAMBRIDGE: W portal and round church, built c. 1100. The N aisle (beyond) was added c. 1350 and the S aisle in 1841. Now that the Temple church in London has been destroyed in the second World War, only three round churches remain in use in England—this, the earliest; that of St. Sepulchre, Northampton, of slightly later date; and that of Little Maplestead, Essex, of c. 1300. The Temple, Northampton, Cambridge and (ruined) Ludlow Castle churches probably arose from the influence of the Crusades. The roof of this church was originally conical. It was changed in the 15C to an octagonal roof with belfry, but in 1841 a roof as like the original as possible was built. There has been much (good) restoration of this church, and the style, buttresses, portal, lantern and corbel-table are authentic.

50 ST. NICHOLAS, OLD SHOREHAM: view from NE. This is the older of the two big churches at Shoreham. The town was once a large seaport, but was diminished by the action of the tides. (See 51, 53 and 56.) There is good stonework in this church, particularly at the W end where Saxon megalithic quoins are situated. It seems to have been built c. 1100 on a simple aisleless cruciform plan with central tower over the crossing, and (like Melbourne, 28) with apsidal ends to transepts and chancel. The chancel was extended in the 13C; but the massive crossing, the break in the N wall of the existing nave, and the remains of a Saxon door there, show that the Norman church incorporated much of the pre-existing 9C or 10C Saxon one, including the base of the Saxon W tower in a new nave. The central tower is a good example of the Franco-Norman style—generally only found in England near the southern sea-coast—with well-defined stages, roundels, and a low-pitched four-gabled roof.

51 ST. MARY DE HAURA, NEW SHOREHAM: view from NW. It shows the W portal in the only surviving (now aisleless) bay of the original nave W of the crossing, the crossing and transepts, the central tower with its Norman lower stage and Transitional to EE upper stage, and the lines of the original roofs of nave and transepts on the faces of this tower. The church, in its original

form, was a colossal edifice for its date: the external length was over 200 ft. The main body of the twin-aisled nave seems to have fallen into ruin in the 17C. The old choir of three equal aisles (now the main body of this parish church) is one of the earliest examples of the Transitional and EE style; it has complex piers and columns to its S arcade, and simpler round columns to the arcade on the N. The E end of the choir externally is very early EE. There are EE flying-buttresses of heavy and early design to N and S of the choir clerestory. For details of the choir piers, capitals, vaulting, etc., and the imposition of Transitional and EE work upon the Norman, see 53, 59. There are on the columns of the N arcade a large number of *graffiti* crosses, signs, and other marks made by master-masons, Templars, Crusaders, travellers and others.

52 ST. MICHAEL, STEWKLEY: view from W, showing tower arches and vaulted square-ended chancel beyond. Like St. Mary, Iffley (31), with which it is always paired, this church was built c. 1150-60, with nave, tower and chancel. The only substantial additions to its Norman style are the EE piscina, sedilia and rood-loft internally, and the P pinnacles to the tower. The W fronts of the tower arches are richly decorated with triple mouldings of, first, beak-heads, cats' heads and grotesques, with tongues overlapping the moulding, and then chevrons. The groined roof of the chancel has ornamented ribs; there is a fine external triple-arch E arcade with central Norman light; and the W front, similarly, has a triple arcade with the portal in the centre and a window above.

53 ST. MARY DE HAURA, NEW SHOREHAM: view from NE end of choir, looking diagonally across to E face of S transept, showing round and octagonal single columns of N arcade and complex piers of S arcade beyond. The transition from pseudo-Corinthian to Gothic foliated capitals can be seen, as well as the Transitional and EE type of wall-shaft (extreme left of picture) to carry the new stone vaulting of the roof. See also 51 and 59.

54 ST. PETER, CASSINGTON: view from W, looking through Norman tower arches into vaulted chancel. It shows arches of two orders and twin-shafts aside, choir, 14C carved rood-screen, deeply recessed D window in N wall beyond pulpit, lower level of original roof, plain Norman cylindrical font, stone-flagged floor, and old

carved 15C benches. The church is Norman, c. 1120, aisleless, with nave, central tower, and square-ended chancel. 14C N and S porches cover Norman portals: in 1318 Lady Montacute raised the Norman tower and superimposed a delicate EE spire. Outside, the Norman corbel-table and a good early 14C one beneath the parapet at the base of the spire remain. Emblems of the Passion are painted on the inside of the S door. The altar rails are *tempore* Charles I.

55 STS. PETER AND PAUL, CHALDON: painting on W wall, c. 1200. It shows "the ladder of salvation", a concept which suggests that the artist must have worked to an Eastern model. In the lower panel are the causes and wages of sin, including the tree of knowledge on the extreme right; in the upper, the triumph of Christ and the blessed. The dedication cross below the frame on the left belongs to the church itself and antedates the painting. The whole forms the finest complete example in England of so early a work. The church is Norman and incorporates in this W wall and its quoins parts of the earlier Saxon church. This apparently went back to the 8C or 9C, and may have had a W tower into which a tall, narrow Saxon opening in the present W wall penetrated. There is (in the porch) a fine church bell, possibly of the 12C, with 12C flower-pot shape and Roman lettering; a (rare) Commonwealth oak pulpit dated 1657; and a (rare) Norman font composed of a monolithic bowl in an octagonal shaft.

56 ST. NICHOLAS, OLD SHOREHAM: view from N side of nave, looking across crossing to SE pier, showing (rare) late 13C wooden rood-screen before chancel, and (rare) Norman tie-beam carved with billet-decoration over W arch of crossing. See 50.

57 ST. BARTHOLOMEW THE GREAT, LONDON: Prior Bolton's early 16C window (his rebus, a "bolt and tun" below it, in the quatrefoil centre-section) and triforium and S arcade from N aisle. The church, founded by King Henry I's jester, Rahere, was built c. 1123-33 and is therefore the oldest parish church in London. It is only the choir of the original priory of Austin Canons —together with the first bay of the original nave and remnants of the transepts. Triforium, clerestory (with later Transitional arches) and ambulatory remain. The central tower is not square; the arches are Transitional,

two rounded and two pointed, and their mouldings are later. Happily, as there are chairs and no pews, the full extent of the Norman walls and piers can be seen from floor to ceiling (see 58). The founder's, Rahere's, tomb with its early 15C groined canopy is on the N of the choir (see 58). There is a notable alabaster tomb of Sir Walter Mildmay (1589); a bust of James Rivers (1641) said to be by Le Sueur; a good 15C screen under the N transept arch; and Sir Henry Wotton's famous couplet on John Whiting:

> "Shee first deceased, he for a little try'd
> To live without her, lik'd it not and dy'd."

58 ST. BARTHOLOMEW THE GREAT, LONDON: view from S aisle of choir, looking across to Rahere's early 15C tomb in N aisle, showing Norman piers, aisles and triforium, Transitional clerestory (with ambulatory in it), and quality of masonry. See 57.

59 ST. MARY DE HAURA, NEW SHOREHAM: view from N arcade, looking up to Transitional triforium and clerestory. It shows springing of roof-vaulting and original Norman E arch of crossing and roof-level (lower right). See 51 and 53.

60 ST. MARY, BIBURY: view from chancel, looking through part-Saxon chancel-arch to Norman and EE N arcade, P roof and W window. Saxon pilaster-strips run up the N and S sides of the nave, and the jambs of the chancel-arch (shown here) are Saxon (the arch itself and the inset moulding in the soffit are EE); there is also a Scandinavian carved stone on the outside of the chancel N wall, and others were sent to the British Museum in 1913 (copies preserved). The church has a good Norman N door with a later (rare) trefoiled tympanum. Aisles were thrown out in the 12C, and in the 13C the nave was extended and the chancel lengthened to the E; a fine EE square font dates from that period. In the chancel there are examples of the problematical "low side-windows", EE lancets, and, on the S, a very small rectangular window with 13C glazing. The church antedates the late 14C development of the wool trade in the Cotswold region, so we find little 14C D work here. See also 194.

61 ST. MICHAEL, BLEWBURY: 12C Transitional to EE "false" crossing. View from E end of N aisle, looking SE through chancel-arch into S aisle of 12C Transitional

chancel. This crossing is "false" since no transepts exist; it is composed of the vault and four arches of the original Norman-Transitional central tower, now destroyed; the existing W tower is P. There are squints on either side of this chancel-arch, that on the N (here seen) being original Transitional, and that on the S being P with a foliated head. The S aisle is 15C, and the S nave arcade has five Transitional arches, of which the two to the W differ from the others. The N aisle is 14C, with D windows, and the N arcade has D arches.

62 ST. MARY, WEST WALTON: detached EE tower and, beyond, EE S porch, nave roof and clerestory. The Ile de France Gothic is traceable in this kind of EE work, especially in the S tower. The great stride forward from Norman or Transitional work is apparent: in the more delicate arcading of this detached tower and the S porch of the church beyond; in the banding and moulding of the capitals of the more graceful shafts; in the rounded abaci over capitals; and in the arcading and multiplication of lights in windows. This church was built c. 1225-50 with long nave and N and S aisles, S porch, chancel, and detached tower to SE. The N aisle was widened later and has blocked the clerestory lights. The tower is open-arched on all sides at the base, with octagonal buttresses from base to top, and with rich courses, niches, arcading and mouldings. There is a noble S porch (see 68). There is also a fine W door, which is, however, spoiled by big, ugly buttresses added later to support the outward-leaning W wall and W pier of the nave. The N aisle is wider than the nave. The nave arcades have cluster-columns with detached and banded Purbeck shafts and beautifully carved capitals "which vie with the carving in Lincoln cathedral", which is of slightly earlier date (73). There were similar arcades also in the chancel, but they have been blocked and filled; the noble chancel-arch, however, remains. On each side of the sanctuary are (rare) fourfold sedilia. The EE clerestory is continuous, the lights occurring in every third arch of the arcading over it (here visible); but these lights are now blocked on the N and partly so on the S. There is a fine 15C roof. See 68, 73 and 79.

63 ST. GILES, BREDON: view from SE, showing the EE S chapel, the Norman W turret-buttress, EE tower-base and D spire. The Brandons gave a notable survey and engraving of this church over a century ago, and

Rickman made an engraving of the Norman W turret (see Bibliographical Note, p. 22). The church developed from a Norman plan of nave, central tower and chancel, and contains the original Norman N porch, two W turrets, windows at the W end, and W tower-arch inside. About 1230 the lovely EE Mitton chapel was thrown out to the S (see 82). Between 1300 and 1320, the chancel was extended, the central tower raised and the spire added. Thus the church shows both late EE and early D features. The N aisle is D, c. 1350, and there is a P window of c. 1450 at the W end. There is early 14C glass in the chancel windows; an impressive Easter sepulchre; a number of fine tombs (see 82); and a series of (rare) altar steps inset with 14C heraldic encaustic tiles.

64 ST. MARY, UFFINGTON: EE gabled porch on E of S transept. This is a rare 12C EE cruciform church. The central tower has a square base and 18C octagonal upper stage and pinnacles. It is much earlier than West Walton (62), was built c. 1175-1200, and contains many rare features: sexfoiled round window over blocked N door; three square-ended, steep-pitched, gabled, narrow chapels—one to E of N transept, two to E of that on the S (see 67); moulded circles for consecration crosses; EE oak doors and iron-work; strongly moulded string-courses round the whole building; and a finely moulded S door, which Rickman thought was of c. 1220. There are some old 16C bench-ends; two other triangular-gabled portals besides that shown here; and a large D window on the S.

65 ST. JOHN THE BAPTIST, INGLESHAM: view from S porch, looking across aisles and nave through N door, showing EE piers, D screen, and Arabesque N door and frame. See 11 and 70.

66 ST. NICHOLAS, NEW ROMNEY: view from E end of N aisle, looking across to Norman W arcades (right), D arcades to E of them, and S aisle. The church is a fine example of EE and D development, superimposed on a basic Norman design (c. 1100) which ends where the pulpit appears, between the last Norman pier and the first of the D piers. The Norman W tower (with P topmost stage) was added later. It carried beacons, as Romney was one of the Cinque Ports, and ships used to tie up to the churchyard walls. In the 13C to 14C D period the church was extended and the aisles thrown

out. These are (rare) of the same length as the nave and, like it, have altars and chancels, of which two are EE and one D, with sedilia and aumbries to each. The wooden screen at the W end and on the E face of the tower-base is a fine example of its time, marked 1662. There are notably fine tombs, including that (table-tomb, 1622) around which the "jurats" gather to elect the mayor in the S aisle. From earliest times this church was used for municipal, juridical and other secular purposes.

67 ST. MARY, UFFINGTON: N transept showing the pair of narrow chapels with their triple lancets on its E face, the "low side-window" on the N face of the N of the two chapels (right, beside buttress of E wall and N wall of transept), triple lancets on N wall of transept, and roundel below moulding of sill of same window for dedication cross. All of this, except the lantern to the tower, is EE. See 64.

68 ST. MARY, WEST WALTON: S porch, S door within, and arcading of nave clerestory above. See 62. The degree of decay in the masonry can be clearly seen here.

69 ST. MATTHEW, LANGFORD: EE windows, turret-buttresses and cross at W end. See 15.

70 ST. JOHN THE BAPTIST, INGLESHAM: chancel with deeply splayed EE windows, and Norman arcading; EE pier of S arcade and chancel-arch; 17C pulpit; box-pews of 17C and 18C; and 15C screen in N arcade. See 11 and 65.

71 STS. PETER AND PAUL, DORCHESTER: S aisle of nave, Norman lead font, and early D piers, c. 1280–1300. This abbey church is EE and D on a Norman founda-tion. The nave belonged to the people as their church, the rest to the monks, as at Sherborne; and the parish acquired the whole after the Dissolution of the Monas-teries. The S aisle contains the late Norman lead font (see also 43) with cast figures in single arcaded panels; 14C paintings (rood above, and crucifixion above altar); and D piers, one carrying the famous bracket-band of sleeping monks roused by the Devil's horn. The sedilia, parapet, complex cluster-piers, Jesse win-dow (c. 1320), E window, and others in the chancel are outstanding specimens. Rickman devotes many

engravings to piers of different dates, windows (includ-ing a rare early example, c. 1350, of a square-headed P window), capitals, and mouldings in this church.

72 ST. CANDIDA AND HOLY CROSS, WHITECHURCH CANONICORUM: view from S door, looking across nave into N transept to shrine of St. Wite (against N wall of N transept). It shows Transitional font; Norman S and Transitional N arcades; and EE chancel-arch, chancel, and E window of N transept in its arcading. St. Wite (wrongly identified with "white") has been trans-literated into St. Candida (cf. Ninian's *Candida Casa* in Galloway = Whitehouse = Whithorn). There are traces of Saxon work (a rosette on S wall of S aisle and other work in tower and walls). The church is cruci-form, but has a P tower at the W end. Built into this are two (?) Saxon carved stone panels, the one on the S side being possibly the earliest stone representation of a ship in England. The ship may refer to "St. Wite", who is usually identified with Ste. Blanche of Brittany. She is said to have been one of the nuns taken by St. Boniface of Wessex into Saxony in the course of his missions; an old document states that one nun was martyred there, and her body brought back and in-terred "twelve miles from Chard", which is roughly the location of this church. The church is one of the best examples of Wessex EE work. There are fine tombs (see 196); *graffiti* of Crusaders' or travellers' crosses on the E jamb of the S door; a rich Jacobean pulpit; a rare E arch to the S aisle, supported on *trompes* built out from the wall; majestic buttresses to the tower; and an arch in the N arcade opposite the S door, which is narrower than the rest and decorated with a double dog-tooth moulding, suggesting that possibly the shrine of the Saint once stood there.

73 ST. MARY, WEST WALTON: view from S door in S aisle, looking NW through EE nave arcades to the EE clerestory arcading and late D font. See 62, 68 and 79.

74 ST. MARY, ST. KATHARINE AND ALL SAINTS, EDING-TON: view of the D monastic church from SW. This is probably the site of the "Aethandun" where Alfred defeated the Danes in 878. This church was founded and built by a native, William de Edington, Bishop of Winchester, 1352–61, who, as Lord Chancellor, made English the language of the law courts. It shows two transitions in many parts: from EE to D, and already from

D to P. The college for "secular priests" was first set up here, and then, in 1358, converted into an Augustinian house for which this was the church. It is cruciform, with massive central tower, nave and aisles, forming (as at Dorchester, etc.) the parish church; the parish altar was under the W arch of the tower, while the monks used the transepts and choir ("monks' choir"). Fine brown and green contemporary glass remains in the clerestory. There are many notable canopied and other tombs; a fine carved early 15C rood-screen; and a famous W front (rare in English churches) with a mixture of Flamboyant and P tracery in the great W window.

75 ST. MARY, STOKE-SUB-HAMDON: view from S. It shows the small Norman lancet and W buttress at W of nave; EE window; large 15C P window over remains of Norman S porch; EE tower with 15C battlement and gargoyles; Norman chancel, corbel-table and buttresses; "low side-window" (originally unglazed but shuttered) at W end of chancel, by buttress; and EE lancets in chancel. The whole church is an example of an original aisleless, porchless, transeptless and towerless Norman building of c. 1100, with N transept added c. 1225, and S transept c. 1300. The E wall and window are of the 15C; the altar is Jacobean, and the chancel-arch Norman. The N transept has a ribbed vault and fine EE leaf-corbels, with a squint. That on the S has an EE piscina, many EE heads between the windows, four fine EE lancets to N, another squint, and a recessed D tomb. The nave has a (rare) example of a W window with reticulated D tracery; 15C murals; EE piscina; Transitional font; Jacobean pulpit and hour-glass; and a high D or P window on the S to light the rood-loft. The N portal has a famous tympanum of Norman work: Sagittarius bending his bow against the Lion, with an Agnus Dei and a Tree of Life. Some think it to be a representation of King Stephen's victory in 1135 when he usurped the English throne from his cousin Geoffrey of Anjou, Stephen's device being a Sagittarius, and Geoffrey's being the Lion.

76 ST. PANCRAS, ARLINGTON: view from SE. There is a small Saxon double-splay window above the S porch, and "long-and-short" work in the nave quoins. The structure is mainly EE to D, c. 1250-1350; but it conserves a Norman N chapel in the sole N aisle by the EE chancel, and therefore a single arcade of octagonal EE columns, unadorned capitals and arches. The nave roof

is a fine D example with original tie-beams, king-posts and trusses. There are traces of 15C murals; an EE to D font; and many good tombstones and crosses from monastic graves. The flint and rubble coursing (here visible) is a good example of local Kent and Sussex work, in default of Caen or other stone from across the sea.

77 ST. MARY, OTTERY ST. MARY: view from SE. It shows a complete EE (1259) monastic church; (rare) transeptal towers (the only other example in England being Exeter cathedral, from which these were copied); EE buttresses, pinnacles, and remaining lead spire on N tower; single D tower openings; and fine EE and D gables to E of chancel and Lady Chapel. The nave was extended in 1338-42, then the Lady Chapel was built, and the towers were raised in early D style, which harmonized well with the EE work. The college of canons was abolished in 1545, and both then and in the Civil War the church suffered damage. There is an unusual double N arcade, due to the throwing-out of the lovely Dorset aisle with its Tudor fan-tracery, c. 1505-40, on the N. There are also two fine D effigies of the Grandison family under Victorian canopies to the N and S of the N arcades.

78 ST. JOHN THE BAPTIST, BERE REGIS: nave and chancel from P tower at W end, showing Norman font, P carved and painted roof (1470) with figure-trusses and bosses, small P clerestory, (rare) iron grill to large D squint on S of EE chancel-arch, Norman S arcade with hood-mouldings, and fine carved capitals (including one of King John). The S aisle is known as the Turberville chapel because of its connection with Thomas Hardy's "Tess" (see 112); below it is a vast vault where the nuns of Tarrant Abbey, nearby, were buried. Later, that right of burial passed to the Turbervilles whose tombs are set in the E and W walls of this S aisle. The exceptionally fine Norman font, damaged during the Laudian troubles under Charles I (when Laud ordered font-covers to be fitted), should be compared with that at Avebury (45); this font shows the more finished Norman designs and work. The N aisle was Cardinal Morton's chantry chapel. A native of Bere, he gave the roof to this church; the fine W square P tower, with its pinnacled buttresses, was built at the same time. Up to the Dissolution of the Monasteries, the nuns of Tarrant used this aisle, which is higher than

the nave, and thus enabled them to see without being seen. The famous roof includes one boss of the Lancaster rose, 12 figures (supposed to be the Apostles), and painted collars and bosses over all the joints.

79 ST. MARY, WEST WALTON: view from chancel, looking W to D font, double EE W portal, and P W window. It shows roof and tie-beams, EE nave, cluster-columns, clerestory arcading, and chancel-arch. The remains of the EE frame, niches, etc., of the former W window, are also visible. See 62, 68 and 73.

80 ST. MARY, KETTON: view from SE across restored 15C bridge, showing the fine EE spire and Transitional chancel. The church was ruinous by 1232 and was rebuilt in the EE style with a strange overlap of pure Norman details; e.g. the famous W front with its central round-headed portal flanked by narrow and acutely pointed arches, as well as the chancel with Transitional N and S walls and an almost pure EE gable and E end. The EE to D central tower and spire are fine specimens. The various gabled and hooded lights on the cardinal and diagonal faces of the spire, the fine broaching of the octagonal spire on the tower, and the cornices and triple tower-lights are noteworthy.

81 ALL SAINTS, POLEBROOKE: EE tower and spire, and S porch. This really EE spire, which has gabled lights on its cardinal faces only, should be compared with the spires of Ketton (80), Lechlade (107), and Market Harborough (108). The N porch is pure EE. The N and S nave arcades are Transitional; the chancel-arch is Norman; the N transept has fine sedilia round W and N sides; and the rood-screen dates from c. 1400, with traces of original colouring. The fine EE chancel has a triple-light E window (engraved in Rickman), with banded side-shafts and lovely mouldings. There is also a (rare) canopied piscina of c. 1220 (Rickman), and a D roof to the chancel of c. 1320 (Rickman). The corbel-table round the chancel is a fine example of EE work. The contemporary engraving of the tower and W end in Rickman (by Mackenzie and Le Keux) merits examination.

82 ST. GILES, BREDON; Mitton chapel, c. 1230, looking W, showing Reid tomb (1611) and (rare) beautiful trefoil-arcaded EE windows of S wall with (rare) detached shafts. See 63.

83 ST. MICHAEL AND ALL ANGELS, STANTON HARCOURT: chancel, looking towards EE triple-lancet E window in fine EE arcading, and EE triple-lancet S windows with piscina and stone credence ledge on single shaft below. The church is cruciform Norman, with mainly Norman windows. The central tower has been restored, like much of the church; but the rood-screen (see 114) is EE and is one of the earliest examples surviving. In the Harcourt private chapel on the E of the S transept is the Inigo Jones memorial to Sir Philip Harcourt and his first wife. In the S transept is the cast of the statue (in Parliament) of Sir William Harcourt ("We are all Socialists nowadays!") which can be seen in Plate 114. The descent of the Harcourts from "Bernard the Dane" (under Rollo, first Duke of the Normans, when he first invaded Normandy in 876) is shown in the chapel, traced through 40 generations. The tomb of Sir Robert Harcourt, dressed in an early mantle of the Order of the Garter, shows (rare) the Garter on the left leg; it is also one of a pair (the other being at Ewelme in Oxfordshire) showing a woman wearing the Order (here she wears it above the left elbow, whereas at Ewelme it is above the wrist). See 114 and 146.

84 ALL SAINTS, FARINGDON: EE capitals of engaged shafts at crossing (see also 86). This picture with its foliated and floral motifs should be compared with that immediately below (85) which shows the progression to naturalistic figures in D work. The Faringdon church is almost entirely Transitional and EE. Nave, aisles, S porch, central tower over crossing, and transepts are all EE, c. 1200. Round arches, carving of capitals and square abaci in the nave arcades indicate surviving Norman work. The chancel is EE; it has a notable piscina and sedilia; the windows in the N aisle (see 86), as well as the W door, are fine P. The Unton chapel of the N transept has noteworthy tombs and monuments of the 16C.

85 ST. ANDREW, DROITWICH; D or early P capitals of engaged shafts of crossing, with moulded and octagonal abaci above. Compare this naturalistic figure work with the more formal EE work at Faringdon (84). This generally unknown church contains fine work. There are lovely EE lancets, with collared side-shafts and stepped sills, on the N of the N transept-chapel. The present nave is late D or early P, with two aisles. There

are (rare) internal D buttresses, with monuments, supporting the NW pier of the central tower; the nave over the S aisle has queer dormer lights; lily (S) and acanthus (N) cluster-capitals occur on the chancel-arch; and there are corbels (men holding imposts on their shoulders) on the W front of the arch at the E end of the S aisle.

86 ALL SAINTS, FARINGDON: view from EE crossing, looking NW across Transitional N nave arcade and clerestory to aisled N transept. It shows late P windows of N aisle. See 84.

87 ST. ANDREW, EAST HAGBOURNE: view from D N aisle, looking SE to EE chancel-arch and arcade from choir into S aisle. It shows P choir clerestory, D corbels, and part of P pulpit. The church was originally 12C Norman, with chancel and aisleless nave; in the 13C the S aisle, arcade and S chapel (into which S aisle is extended) were thrown out; the old chancel then became the present choir, and a new E chancel was added. The N aisle and N chapel are D, c. 1340. Early in the 15C the S chapel, aisle and W tower were rebuilt. (The nave arch of the original tower remains.) Later in the 15C the nave and chancel walls were raised and clere-stories put in. The chancel, nave roofs and fine E win-dow are also of this time. There are two good timber-framed 15C porches N and S; and a sanctus-bell at the top of the W tower, a rare location.

88 STS. PETER AND PAUL, SALLE (ALSO SALL, SAWL, SAWLE, ETC.): Seven-Sacrament 15C font, cover, and trussed cover-beam or arm. The church is P through-out, one of the best in England, with a fine P nave roof, (rare) panelled transept roofs (from which those of the House of Lords are said to have been copied), and a remarkably graceful and—for the P style—austere E arch of the W tower into the nave (here visible). Doors and windows are largely original; the E window is especially fine; and the (defaced) lower part of the rood-screen, showing parts of the Apostles' creed and painted a rich green colour, still remains. The position of the rood-beam, above, can still be seen. The central bosses of the chancel roof depict the life of Christ; in one, the Resurrection, He is actually stepping on a sleeping sentinel. There is good old glass in the windows; a ringers' gallery in the tower (here shown); a canopy over the chancel-arch; and a 15C pulpit and stalls. The fine W front, c. 1410, has interesting carvings of angels

dressed in feathered "tights", copied from actors in the early miracle-plays; 14 carved shields with emblems, symbols, etc.; and a fine W door. There is a noble P W tower with two P windows in the second and fourth stages, and a (rare) fretted panel-ventilator ("sound hole") in the stage between. The church is a "wool church" in which no less than six guilds had their altars. The font has been badly defaced, but still shows more of the beauty of these Seven-Sacrament fonts than most of the three dozen remaining in England—of which only two are outside Norfolk and Suffolk.

89 ST. MARY, BAMPTON: view from W end. It shows the EE to D banded spire with gabled lights on the cardinal faces, and P statues with brackets at the base of the spire in place of pinnacles at the diagonals. The church has Saxon herring-bone stonework over the chancel-arch and in the two E piers of the central tower. There is some "long-and-short" work at the foot of the central tower, which reinforces the supposition that the present chancel incorporates a Saxon church. Of cruciform plan, the church has Norman transepts with traces (rare) of apsidal E transeptal chapels; Transitional 12C nave and aisles; E and W windows (the latter shown here) of good D style; late 15C S porch; good 15C misericords and stalls in the chancel; a fine P Easter sepulchre in three tiers, and sedilia, in the chancel; and a unique 14C reredos of Christ and the Apostles, in one piece. There are many *graffiti* crosses and other marks. The S and N doors have rounded trefoil heads, and there are (rare) cinquefoil canopies to the interior of the N and S aisle windows, which produce a lovely effect with the EE to D lancets beyond them. The fine W door is D, c. 1320. Rickman gives good engravings of doors, windows, etc., at Bampton as they appeared over 100 years ago.

90 ST. MARY, ASHWELL: W tower (D to P) and timber lych-gate, from village. Clerestory, chancel-arch and the four bays of the nave from E in this striking monastic church, are of the D style. The chancel, W tower, and W bays of the nave and aisles are D to P, some 30 years later. The great wind of 1361 destroyed the newly built W tower and the two W bays of the nave, which had to be rebuilt. The S porch dates from 1420; the N porch is mid-15C. Only the roof of the S aisle is original. The fine, boldly buttressed W tower is about 176 ft. high, with the "Hertfordshire spike"

spire which took the place of the original battlemented top in 1714. The *flèche* is of wood, on an octagonal drum, and is covered with lead; it bears the raised inscription, in capitals: "Thos Everard / Laid me here / he said to l(ast) / an hundred / year / 1714." The N wall of the tower internally has rare and remarkably artistic *graffiti* referring to the ravages of the Black Death in 1349–50. One of them is an incised drawing of a large church with double transepts, lofty central tower, and spire—which seems to incorporate both the tower of Old St. Paul's, London, and the transepts of Westminster Abbey. The open-timber lych-gate (just visible here) is apparently also of the mid-15C.

91 ST. EDITH, COATES-BY-STOW: S wall of nave and chancel, showing W bellcote, Norman S portal, blocked priests' door and P windows. This is an isolated, little-known gem of a rural Norman church with simple rectangular nave and chancel only. See immediately following Note for details of the interior.

92 ST. EDITH, COATES-BY-STOW: view of nave and 15C rood-screen, looking E, showing thickness of Norman walls, 15C tie-beam, P windows, 15C bench-ends and plain Norman tub-font. The 15C pulpit can just be seen; the rood-screen has wooden vaulting on the side of the nave (also visible); and the rood-gallery remains. There is also a perfect rood-stair on the S side, and faint traces of the Virgin on the rood-loft are still visible. The original stone altar with its six consecration-crosses remains (rare, because of the order of 1550 to take them down and install communion tables).

93 ST. NICHOLAS, BAULKING: nave from SW, looking through (rare) EE stone screen to chancel. This is a simple nave-and-chancel 13C EE church, like that (earlier) described in the two immediately preceding Notes. It has a good triple lancet at the E end; four side lancets; and a beautiful (rare) angle-piscina with central shaft and openings N and W (reminiscent of that at nearby North Moreton, which has triple shafts and is dated c. 1320 by Rickman). The stone screen is exceptional; it rises only to the height of the chancel walls (the fine Berkshire-barn-like roof can be seen extending over it); the chancel-arch in it is EE; but the squints (single to N, double to S) are probably of a later date. The pulpit here shown is Jacobean; the font is probably

EE; and there is a small wooden bellcote at the W end. The tie-beam over the pulpit shows the date 1708.

94 ST. ANDREW, BUGTHORPE: view from SW, showing pinnacled P W tower and D Chapel beyond original chancel. The original structure seems to have consisted of a Saxon nave and chancel only. The nave now runs to a chancel-arch which appears Transitional, but springs from complex imposts, some of which show a Saxon, others a Norman interlacing type of carving. The fine D chapel beyond the old chancel has a turret (just visible here), splendid D windows, and D buttresses. There is a low EE arch from the W tower into the nave, and an EE font.

95 ST. LAWRENCE, NORTH HINKSEY: view from SE, showing "stepping" downhill from 13C W tower; late 17C or early 18C S porch; EE chancel with EE lancet above "low side-window" in S wall; and base and shaft of churchyard cross. The original 12C walls of the nave largely remain. The S door is mid-12C, of two orders. The original Norman chancel-arch was very narrow and about 8 ft. high, but the entire stone screen and arch was rebuilt last century.

96 ST. LAWRENCE, BESSELSLEIGH: S porch and W bellcote. This was originally a 12C church with simple nave and chancel, of which the W wall remains; the chancel was extended in the 13C; the windows are of the 13C, 14C and 15C. The wooden screen was inserted in 1632, when the S porch and bellcote here shown were probably also built. The E chancel and W nave windows are early D or late EE; the E window, however, has a fine inner cinquefoil arch reminiscent of Bampton (see 89). The rood-stair remains on the N side.

97 ST. MARGARET, CLEY: trefoiled and cusped ogee D S door in vaulted porch, looking into nave to P Seven-Sacrament font. (See the immediately following Plate, which shows the reverse view through this door and porch, and the font in better detail.) The D motifs persisted well into the 15C in Norfolk. The exterior of the porch has fine heraldic work, a niche for St. Margaret, and a sundial.

98 ST. MARGARET, CLEY: S nave arcade, and S door, showing defaced 15C carved Seven-Sacrament font,

D clerestory, and corbel of dancing minstrel with pipe and tabor between arches. The cusped D windows (P in the S aisle) are outstanding. The church shows a steady progression of all styles from c. 1250. In the 14C and 15C transepts were thrown out and the aisles (which were D) were raised and altered to take P windows, N and S porches, etc. The floor of the nave is tiled with lovely square tiles from the Low Countries, given in exchange for East Anglian wool. There are (rare) *graffiti* of ships, probably scratched by sailors (as also at Blakeney, 101); and there is original glass in the tracery of the S aisle window here shown. On the S side of the nave by the chancel there is a good example of the humour of the age; an imp with a glass eye appears to be winking at certain pews. There are also a Jacobean pulpit; old oak 15C stalls and misericords in the chancel; a lovely geometrical Arabesque window in the S wall of the S transept; and a splendid early 16C brass to John and Agnes Symonds and their eight children.

99 HOLY TRINITY, LITTLEBURY: EE nave arcades and tower-arch. The N aisle is c. 1225, and the S transept and S aisle were merged c. 1250; the W tower is c. 1325. The W arches of the nave arcades are somewhat wider than the rest. There is a Transitional font in fine Tudor linenfold wood casing with doors, engraved hinges, and pinnacled cover. See also 171.

100 ALL SAINTS, SUTTON COURTENAY: Norman W tower and nave-arch from E, showing 14C D nave arcades with tie-beam roof, and 12C Transitional font with narrow arcades. The chancel was rebuilt and extended in the 13C; but the E arch of the S nave arcade shows embattled and chevron mouldings of the 12C springing from a 13C pillar! The fine red-brick S porch is early 16C with a chamber above. The wine-glass pulpit is 17C; the old pews (here shown) are early 15C; and the royal arms of Charles II appear over the chancel-arch. There are an early 15C screen and stalls in the chancel, and a (rare) 14C altar-tomb in the churchyard S of the chancel.

101 ST. NICHOLAS, BLAKENEY: P towers, W to left and NE to right. The smaller, to NE, was a lantern for mariners. The church, as striking in many details as Cley (98), has a lovely EE chancel with stone vaulting and (rare) seven grouped EE lancets as an E window

(scarcely visible here behind the summer foliage). It has a fine 15C P font carved with figures of saints and emblems on the bowl; and a typically rich W tower with intermediate square ventilator-panel, fretted as at Salle (88) and miscalled a "sound-hole". The nave has a noble hammer-beam roof. There are a good Easter sepulchre and a restored 15C screen and rood-loft.

102 ST. ANDREW, BRAMFIELD: view from SE, showing detached W round tower and 14C D nave and chancel windows. The church has a simple nave and chancel with later S porch; it was built some 150 years after the tower. The latter, of coursed flint and rubble 5 ft. thick, runs up to a later red-brick top course, and has lights suggesting a date c. 1175–1200; but it is possible that it was only rebuilt then and that the base is of the 11C. The church is famous for its superb carved and painted wooden rood-screen (see 106), a mural of angels in an arched recess on the N wall of the nave, fine Rabett and Nelson tombstones in the chancel, and the Coke monument (see 199).

103 ST. JOHN THE BAPTIST, TUNSTALL: view from SW, showing typical northern P massive structure, battlementing, buttresses, etc. See also 104, immediately following. These are typically large northern parishes, which owe their size to the lower density of population and the difficulty of communications. For details of this church see 7.

104 ST. CUTHBERT, GREAT SALKELD: defensive W tower built c. 1380, Norman nave and P chancel, from NW. This region was even more perilous for its inhabitants, during the Border raids of cattle-barons and other freebooters, than that near Tunstall (103). The massive W tower was defensive, for the place had twice been laid waste by the Scots before 1380, and there is a roomy dungeon under the tower. The Norman nave was built c. 1080, doubtless also as a defensive outpost, and there is a fine S door with the sun, bee, serpent and other Scandinavian emblems treated in Norman fashion. The place was abandoned in the Scottish-English wars. In 1480 the P chancel was built and the Norman nave walls were raised and new windows inserted.

105 ST. MARY, DENNINGTON: 15C carved and painted wooden parclose screen with gallery above, round Bardolf chapel in S aisle, with Bardolf alabaster effigies

42

and Rous wall-monument. This chantry-chapel—and screen—is matched by that of St. Mary on the N. The magnificent 13C and 14C church has a fine D window in the E of the D chancel; stained glass in chancel windows; a hanging pyx in the sanctuary; an early 15C open timber roof; a remarkable collection of 15C carved benches with poppyheads (see 119), one of which shows the mythical one-footed "Sciapus" or "Sciapod"; Georgian "family-pews" in front of these; a fine three-decker Caroline pulpit; and notable buttresses and a flushwork-panelled N porch outside. The beautiful screen formerly continued across the nave as a rood-screen, but has been destroyed. The W tower is a fine example of flintwork with massive buttresses of open-joint flint and stonework. See also 119 and 159.

106 ST. ANDREW, BRAMFIELD: P rood-screen from SW, showing Coke monument (199) in chancel beyond (see 102). The carving of the screen shows tracery and ribs of a late date, and both the door and the heads of the side panels suggest Tudor treatment. The painting of detail on panels, heads and vaulting is exquisite, with a wealth of gold and bright colours.

107 ST. LAWRENCE, LECHLADE: embattled W tower, with pinnacles and spire, built c. 1490, reputedly by the vicar Conrad Ney and the parishioners. The P style conserves something of the D here, e.g. the banded spire. The church has a chancel, nave, aisles and a fine N porch, but Victorian restoration (1882–8) has left rather a heavy mark on it. One of the roof bosses shows wrestlers (rare).

108 ST. DIONYSIUS, MARKET HARBOROUGH: late EE to D steeple (c. 1300), at W end of P nave (c. 1480–1520). According to tradition, the church was founded by John of Gaunt, and is one of only five in England dedicated to the Areopagite. The steeple is typical of the Leicestershire-Northamptonshire kind, with a liberal use of crockets, a fine broach from the octagon to the square of the tower, quatrefoil and other arcading, drip-courses, mouldings, stout and frequently set-off corner-buttresses, and gabled spire-lights.

109 ST. THOMAS À BECKET, WINCHELSEA: view from NE, showing fine D (but much restored) windows, buttresses, E flying-buttress, and triple-roofed structure. The church is early 14C D, and was planned for a long

nave running W of the W bell-turret (c. 1770); but the nave was never built, and what was begun was destroyed, probably owing to lack of funds after the Black Death. The present nave is the original chancel. The S porch is 16C; so is the present W porch, which is under the original chancel-arch; there is a crypt below the sanctuary; and the many windows—once containing "the finest D work anywhere in Sussex"—have been so often restored since 1850 that they now have a Gothic Revival appearance. The E window was inserted in 1850, replacing one of the 15C. The interior has some of the finest EE and D tombs in England: the three in the N chapel are of the latter half of the 13C; in the S chapel famous Alard tombs, of Caen stone (restored 1905), with crocketed canopies, date from 1315 and 1330. The early D chancel arcades have exquisite mouldings.

110 ST. JAMES, LOUTH: The "superbly graceful", 300 ft. high W tower and spire (P 1501–15), viewed from SE. Many consider this spire second only to that "queen of spires" at Salisbury cathedral; Tyrrell-Green thought it "the most perfect in the kingdom". This church is interesting for many reasons. It is one of the biggest in England, yet still shows the peculiar and paradoxical English fashion of building parish churches on plans and assumptions different from those used for cathedrals; this church, and that at Ludlow (131), for example, are far more imposing outside than in, whereas with English cathedrals the opposite is the case. The spire is richly crocketed, as are most in the Lincolnshire-Leicestershire-Rutland-Northamptonshire stone area; flying-buttresses connect the spire with ornate pinnacles; ogee arches are employed at ground-level and in the fourth stage of the tower proper, but spire-lights are smaller and fewer than in the earlier styles. The interior of the church is mainly of good early P style, except for the much older tower-base (130). There is a fine E end and E window with P tracery. The D nave arcades probably belonged to an earlier church; at least two others were on this site; and older N and S doors have been incorporated in the present structure.

111 ST. MORWENNA, MORWENSTOW: view from SE. It shows triple roof over nave and aisles covering inner West Country waggon roofs, W tower with P top and pinnacles (on earlier base), and the typical English crowding of graves on the S side, away from "the

Devil's side" (N). St. Morwenna was one of the "chil-dren" of that famous King Brychan (Brecon) who sent so many saints across the seas from Wales to the Celtic lands of England and Brittany in the Dark Age of the 5C. The church (best known, perhaps, by reason of R. S. Hawker's novel *The Vicar of Morwenstow*) has a Norman or Saxon font with crude cable-carving; a good Norman S door; three Norman piers in the N arcade of the nave, with two Transitional-EE piers to the E of these; a P arcade on the S; and good typical Cornish carved benches with square P ends. It has such a commanding view of the sea (here shown) that for a long time the church tower was, and still is, a landmark.

112 ST. GREGORY, MARNHULL: view from E. This is the church of a village made famous by *Tess of the d'Urber-villes*. It is aisled, triple-roofed, and cruciform, with a fine D tower to the W which was restored in 1718 with a Georgian parapet and pinnacles. Inside, the N arcade (second pier from E) shows Transitional remains; the N arcade is EE; the transept arches are D; and the new S arcade (1852) and S aisle were kept in the D style, like the (original) chancel-arch itself. The W window of the N aisle is EE, but the E window was left un-finished (possibly because of the Black Death in 1348). The chancel is Victorian (1881). The font is probably made of a standing-cross stone for a bowl, on a D Pur-beck pillar from another font. The royal arms over the S door are misleading; they are Stuart, but the ascrip-tion is Georgian.

113 ST. BOTOLPH, HADSTOCK: view from NE (see 6), showing 14C and 15C additions on N; 15C W tower; and chancel of 1884.

114 ST. MICHAEL AND ALL ANGELS, STANTON HARCOURT: view from chancel, looking through EE chancel screen into S transept and along S wall of nave. It shows mould-ings of EE crossing capitals, and the plaster cast of the statue of Sir William Vernon Harcourt, now in Parliament (see 83 and 146). The holes in the lower part of the screen were probably made much later and serve no ritual purpose. The wood arcading is rare.

115 ST. WENDREDA, MARCH: P carved and double-hammer-beamed timber roof, c. 1450. This is the most strikingly ornate of its kind in England. Apostles, saints and angels support brackets, decorate truss-ends, and flank roof-bosses. "The fluttering wings of the angel host spread all over the roof of the church caught the imagina-tion of the people, and this scheme was repeated in many grand timber roofs, as at Wymondham, Cawston . . ." (Gardner's *English Medieval Sculpture*; see Biblio-graphical Note, p. 23, and for Cawston see 144 and 154.) The D church has a finely panelled flint-flush-work clerestory outside; the W tower is not engaged, but stands on arches to make way for a passage through the base (see Warwick, 197). Otherwise it is a typical East Anglian long-naved building.

116 HOLY TRINITY, BALSHAM: carved late 14C D to P choir-stalls and misericords. The church is mainly P; the late D to P chancel was built 1390–1400 and "stalled with twenty-one stalls of good oak" by Rector John Sleford who died 1400. He is buried, by the lovely screen he gave, in the middle of the chancel under an outstandingly fine engraved brass. The handsome screen and rood-loft remain, together with some fine 15C brasses. As at March (115), the cost of maintaining this typically rich East Anglian fabric is far in excess of the capacity of the modern parish. The two churches exemplify the effect of the diversion of trade and riches from medieval East Anglia—though the problem is now the same in every rural English parish with a sub-stantial church.

117 ST. PETER, OUNDLE: 15C brass lectern and painted wooden pulpit. Massive 13C nave pillars of an earlier church remain; and there is a 13C EE N door, a three-light E window in the N transept with ball-flower decoration in D style, a W window in the N aisle of fine 13C lancets with embryonic tracery, and a grand EE five-lancet window in the S aisle (c. 1200), nicely engraved in Rickman. The chancel-arch, transept arches and columns are of the 14C, but they have 12C plinths. The wooden screens round the chancel are of the 15C. The fine S porch is of c. 1485; the early P W tower has buttresses at all four corners—showing that it was built separately—and a striking crocketed spire, 210–215 ft. high, rebuilt in 1634. This has often been climbed by boys of Oundle School, though the crockets are a yard apart and afford poor handhold. There are several good examples of EE, D and P lancets, tracery, mouldings and string-courses at Oundle, many of which are engraved in Rickman.

118 STS. PETER AND PAUL, PICKERING: 15C frescoes on N wall of nave, showing 15C clerestory and Norman N arcade. The frescoes, discovered in 1851, depict (invisible in the Plate) St. George and St. Christopher, the latter generally placed opposite the S door for travellers to invoke before their journeys; next (above, to left of the clerestory window in our picture) the coronation of the Virgin; below that, Herod's feast with Salome dancing, John beheaded (left), and John warning Herod (centre); and, over the next spandrel, the martyrdom of St. Thomas à Becket (above) and the martyrdom of St. Edmund at the hands of the Danes in 870 (below). There are also frescoes on the S wall, but not on so bold a scale. The S aisle was added c. 1200, and the S arcade shows both Transitional and EE piers. An EE square-ended chancel replaced the apsidal Norman one, and was widened; a fine EE S porch, large enough for services and secular business, was added, and the EE to D W tower built and its spire added. In the chancel there is a tablet to the memory of two surveyors from Pickering who helped L'Enfant survey Washington, D.C., early last century. There are brasses commemorating Walter Hines Page, American Ambassador at the Court of St. James in World War I, and the American-British alliance in that war; panelling contributed by (inter alios) Mrs. W. H. Page and the Choate family (in memory of another American Ambassador); and heraldic arms of the U.S.A. on the priests' stalls. There are also a Hepplewhite 18C pulpit, and a fine (rare) belfry screen of the 16C at the base of the W tower. The font is possibly Saxon, and was deliberately defaced (and so recorded in the registers) in 1644.

119 ST. MARY, DENNINGTON: 15C carved bench-ends and poppyheads, and 18C box-pews. The pews are notably more comfortable in an age when preaching had become important. The benches have narrow seats and vertical backs, but at the time when they were built sermons were short and there was much movement about the church for ritual purposes. See 105 and 159.

120 ST. MARY, WORSTEAD: W tower and S side of late D (or early P) church (1370–1400) from SW. It shows flint-and-ashlar flushwork panels on buttresses, etc., typical East Anglian rose-carved fretted ventilator-panels on tower faces, looped and battlemented tower-parapet (1861), crocketed pinnacles, and original late D window tracery. As already noted (Salle, 88) the D style was protracted in Norfolk. Worstead, which is now only a little village, gave its name to the famous cloth and was in the 13C, 14C and 15C heyday of the East Anglian woollen trade one of the wealthiest towns in a wealthy region. The fine S porch is later than the rest, with P vaulting and crocketed niches over the portal. There is also a typically noble East Anglian P carved and painted rood-screen, and (rare) a splendid Gothic Revival (1831) P style W screen with original (1501) inscribed wooden gallery above, in the E arch into the nave from the W tower (see Cawston, 144 and 154), which seems to have replaced one earlier. (One of the three handsome lithographs of the church in the Brandons' 1848 volume, *Parish Churches*, shows font and W screen through the rood-screen from the E.) There are also a good octagonal panelled stone P font with typical heavy suspended cover of East Anglian tabernacle-work; flying buttresses aside at the E of the nave externally (later), just visible in this picture beyond the S porch roof; fine late D mouldings and panelling of flint and stone, enriched with quatrefoils, all round the base of tower and church; (later) P hammer-beam roof with fine tracery in the spandrels; (later) P clerestory; good N and S aisle-screens, carved and painted (but badly restored in the 19C); and some fine niches for statues in the church. The church is an object-lesson to ecclesiologists and ordinary visitors: Neale (a native of the place) and Le Keux in *Collegiate and Parochial Churches* (1823–4) describe the font as hexagonal, which is wrong but has been frequently copied by other authors; Cotman accurately drew both N and S porches in 1817, but among his etchings of that date appears one of "Worsted Screen" which was published in 1838 with Rickman's text, yet has nothing to do with Worstead, and must have been due to a slip in Cotman's notes; the Gothic Revival W screen, and 19C heavy-handed restorations of the woodwork and (above all) the paintings on the older and finer screens in nave and aisles, mislead many people, for many of their subjects have absolutely no relevance to the vanished originals; and, finally, in Neale's text of 1823 the carved date of the W tower gallery (over the 19C screen) is given as MCCCCCL instead of MCCCCCI, post-dating the woodwork half a century. Jewitt and Mackenzie engraved the font and W screen in the fifth and later editions of Rickman.

121 ST. MARY, HUISH EPISCOPI: W tower of 15C P style. It shows open tracery of parapet combined with battlement, and extra pinnacles on corbels at angles and midway; pinnacles to double buttresses at each of three setoffs, etc.; and pierced stone tracery for the double belfry windows. It is a notable tower, typical of the Somersetshire towers (see Tickhill 148, and Worstead 120, for comparison and contrast). Their splendour is attributed to architectural specialists supported by the famous Abbey of Glastonbury, to the fine local stone which nurtured such artists—as in Purbeck—and to the support Henry VII gave in gratitude to Somerset men for their loyalty to his cause in the Wars of the Roses. The church has a fine late Norman S door with elaborately carved columns and capitals, of which the local stone is reddened by fire; the tympanum is missing, and the space has been filled with shaped and keyed stones (later). There is a good Jacobean pulpit, dated 1625. The glass at the E of the S aisle is by Burne-Jones.

122 ALL SAINTS, MARTOCK: P roof and clerestory (1513). This should be compared with the earlier (c. 1450) East Anglian angel-roof at Blythburgh, 123. There was an earlier church of the 13C and 14C at Martock, of which large stone masonry remains. There is a fivefold set of EE lancets at the E end; and the chancel is (rebuilt) EE. The Cromwellians destroyed the statues and old paintings in the niches under the trusses of the splendid tie-beamed roof (here shown) but at the Restoration the saints were repainted and are curious examples of late 17C work. There is a Sanctus bellcote on the E gable of the nave; and the font is octagonal, of the 15C. On the N side of the W tower outside there is a fives-court; the players damaged the buttresses by cutting fives-tallies into them, and cut steps up to the roof to retrieve the balls.

123 HOLY TRINITY, BLYTHBURGH: P painted tie-beamed angel-roof. Compare and contrast this roof with that (later) at Martock, 122. Cromwell's men are said to have stabled their horses in the church and so broken the floor; they tried to shoot down the angels and figures of the roof, and succeeded in places (as here shown), leaving a large number of rents and bullet-holes. The wood-carvings of the P bench-ends are famous: particularly the bench-end-head figures representing the Seven Deadly Sins and Occupations of the Months. There is also a fine Jacobean pulpit and double lectern;

magnificent carved choir-stalls with figures and emblems; a (rare) 15C poor-box; remarkable old tombs and brasses; and a Seven-Sacrament font damaged by both lightning and the Puritans. The church is noteworthy for its fine flint flushwork panels, buttresses, size and number of nave and clerestory windows, lovely S porch (compare that at Worstead, 120), intricate parapet to S aisle, and statues as pinnacles to buttresses (for all of which see 155). It is today another sad relic of the former riches of East Anglian seaports which carried on the wool trade with the Low Countries.

124 ST. ANDREW, CULLOMPTON (ALSO COLLUMPTON, ETC.). 24-bay P painted and carved cradle-roof, top of rood-screen, tie-beam with royal arms above, and nave and chancel arcades and clerestory (see also 129 and 141). This is one of the richest of the famous P West Country wool churches. The noble S Lane chapel (see 129 and 141) and rich W tower are of a later date, being 1520–26 and 1546. The plan is typical of the West Country churches: almost rectangular, with aisles and no chancel-arch. The nave is of great height; and there is a noble Jacobean W gallery running the full width of this wide church (rare). On the E face of the full-length splendidly carved P rood-screen (c. 1450–75), with its early fan-tracery vaulting, is the original painting; the W face was repainted in 1849. There are fine N and S carved oak parcloses to the chancel aisles (see also 105), and an octagonal P font. The W tower (see 129) shows rich decoration. It has massive double-buttresses, each with four double set-offs and canopied niches above; many grotesques; a defaced rood above a lower W window; in that window, arms of Edward VI and the bishop under whose aegis the tower was built; statues of the King and St. George flanking the window; a clock dated 1685 and set in an almost Rococo Gothic frame; a fine P belfry window, mullioned, and transomed into two upper and two lower lights; an ornate embattled and pierced parapet, with quatrefoils and typical mid-wall pinnacles on corbels (see also 121); and a fine oak W door in a deeply moulded W portal.

125 ST. MARY, SAFFRON WALDEN: W end of P nave arcades. It shows E face and buttresses (with set-offs) of (earlier) W tower; incomplete W arches of nave;

1660 royal arms of Charles II; trussed P roof of c. 1480; and piers, pilasters, buttresses and spandrels of nave arcades of c. 1475 (compare Martock 122, which has no such buttresses). This imposing church, in what was an old Saxon village and then a rich wool town, took the place in the latter half of the 15C of an early D church, which was cruciform with central tower. Under the three E windows of the N aisle remain some 14C late D and early P carvings of ritual and Biblical subjects in twelve mullioned recesses. As at Blyth-burgh (123) and Ashwell (90), a great storm seems to have led to rebuilding: first of the chancel, c. 1450; then of the W tower, c. 1470; then, c. 1475-1526, effecting junctions at both ends which are still visible, of the new P nave, with its wider aisles, panelled clere-story, and (rare) Tudor turrets at the E ends. The W tower was finished with a wooden spire; but in 1832 Rickman built the fine present crocketed and late D octagonal spire, supported from the Tudor-style pin-nacles by neat flying-buttresses. The roof of the EE chancel is said to have come from another religious building; the two E bays of the fine roof before the chancel-arch are more ornately decorated, to form a ceiling over the vanished rood and screen. N and S aisles are as wide as the nave, each being similarly roofed with tie-beams on long brackets. A good N porch of c. 1500 has fine vaulting and bosses, and the S porch (rather earlier) has fan-vaulting. There are fine tombs, especially the 1544 Audley tomb of black Belgian slate.

126 ST. JOHN THE BAPTIST, ST. MARY AND ST. LAWRENCE, THAXTED: D nave and arcades, and P N aisle, from chancel, showing low-pitched trussed roof of c. 1510, soffits of Tudor clerestory arches, N nave arcade, and late P window of N aisle. This parish church, like that at Saffron Walden, is one of the largest and finest in the country; and, similarly, it stands on an old and high site. The dedication of St. Lawrence refers to the patron saint of the cutlers (for whom the town was once renowned), whose fine 15C Guild Hall stands below the church. It is also a wool church. The crocketed P spire of the W tower rises to 181 ft. It was rebuilt in 1822. The present nave arcades are those of the earlier D church. The S transept, aisle and porch are early P (1360-80); the N transept is of 1400; the widened N aisle and N porch are of c. 1445; the W tower is of c. 1485; and the chancel, chancel chapels (with their rare pierced

spandrels), clerestory, and roof of nave, are of c. 1510. The chancel bears the emblems of Edward IV, in whose reign it was finished. There are an early 15C reredos in the N transept; stained glass of the 14C and 15C; a rare P 15C font-case and doors; fine D portrait heads on nave arches; and a good 16C pulpit. There are painted ceilings to the chancel and chapels, and 17C screens to chapels. Externally there are pinnacled buttresses, gar-goyles, large late P and early Tudor windows, a richly carved N porch, and a simpler, earlier S porch. Among its precious pieces of stained glass are a Mortimer knight; a steersman in a ship (c. 1510) showing the manner of reefing seagoing sails; the Clare arms found also at Ludlow (131), Stanford-in-the-Vale (168) and Black-more (173); and the Mortimer arms, found also at Ludlow (131).

127 ST. PETER, TIVERTON: Greenway chapel and S porch of 1517, showing the 16C ships over the head of the chapel windows; pierced and embattled parapet and pinnacles; label and niches, with carvings, over S porch; and carvings on buttresses, as on the Lane Chapel at Cullompton (141). The church is early 15C P, but incorporates the N doorway of the earlier Norman church. John Greenway, a rich wool merchant, added the chancel-screen, widened the S aisle, and built out the S porch, S front, and chapel. The N aisle is of 1856; the W tower, of c. 1400, has poor, thin pinnacles and buttresses, the latter not being at the corners. The showpiece is the (Greenway) S chapel. It has the arms of England and France (? wool trade) and the Cour-tenay family on the face of the porch; an excellent late P or early Tudor roof; Greenway brasses and tomb; and externally, on or by string-courses, scenes from the Life of Christ, ships of many kinds, emblems of the woolstaplers' trade and their marks, and Greenway bio-graphical details (see Lavenham, and the Spring family's details, 134). The ships are very important; they show details—e.g. cannon—at a date when scarcely half a dozen ships had been sunk by cannon. The development of gun-mountings 'tween-decks, and of the setting of bigger sails, can also be traced.

128 ST. EDMUND KING AND MARTYR, SOUTHWOLD: view from S. It shows the long run of the P S aisle and clere-story windows, the peculiar East Anglian ridge bellcote, and the flint flushwork panels on the buttresses. The function of buttresses, when windows are large and

manifold, is made clear in this picture. This is the finest of the 61 English churches dedicated to the King of East Anglia who was martyred by the Danes (see 118 and 165). In the W end over the door, in crowned flint-and-stone flushwork, is set SCT EDMUND ORA PRO NOBIS. The church has a typical East Anglian plan—nave and chancel are flanked with continuous, well-nigh equal aisles. The typical East Anglian flint-and-stone flushwork is outstanding, especially on the fine P spireless W tower; this has flushwork panels over the W face of the first two stages, up the (angle) buttresses, and round the parapet; and the work extends over the fine (vaulted) 15C S porch (which matches those at Worstead, 120, Cley 97 and 98, Blythburgh 155, Lavenham 134, etc.) This rich wool church also has a Seven-Sacrament font and a (rare) 15C painted pulpit. The glories of this church, apart from its flushwork, are the rood-screen and roof. The full-width 15C screen still retains some of the original painted panels—of rare colour and gesso work; there are paintings of the Nine Orders of Angels, some indistinct now, showing curious variations of dress of the medieval miracle-plays and players (including angels in feathered "tights" like those over the W door at Salle, 88), and others more elaborately clad (as in the Beauchamp chapel at Warwick, 189).

129 ST. ANDREW, CULLOMPTON: 16C W tower and Lane chapel, showing woolstaplers' marks, ship-carvings, etc., on middle stage of chapel buttresses and over heads of windows. See 124 and 141.

130 ST. JAMES, LOUTH: vault of lower portion of P W tower, c. 1450-1500. Compare and contrast this with the earlier D tower and later P vault at Ludlow crossing, in 131. The sun motif in the central boss recurs in many such places; see Muchelney, 195, for a later example. For Louth church, see 110.

131 ST. LAWRENCE, LUDLOW: crossing and D central 15C tower with vaulting. This fine P central tower, on D lower stages, has both main and subordinate pinnacles at the top. It should be compared and contrasted with that of the W tower at Louth, in 130. Ludlow church is one of the biggest parish (formerly collegiate) churches in England, and one of the finest. It is partly of Norman and EE but mainly of D and P, cruciform style, with famous 14C and 15C wood carvings on the aisle-

screens and rood-screen, stalls, misericords and poppy-heads. There are also a large Norman font (rescued from use as a water-trough), good D sedilia and piscina, and a lovely EE window in a small S chamber. The church also has a magnificent (but heavily restored) panelled and carved stone reredos containing (rare) tiers for statues, a (rare) vaulted hexagonal S porch, many big early P windows with transoms, and the chapel of the guild of the fletchers (arrow-makers), whose badge is in the roof in the N transept. In the NE chapel (of the palmers' guild) of the N transept (matching the Lady chapel of that on the S) is a (rare) Tudor baldachino or celure over the altar; and the Lady chapel to the S has a beautiful D "Jesse" window on the E. It may be mentioned here that St. Apollonia, patron saint of sufferers from toothache, appears in a window of Ludlow church (see Ludham, 145); and that the ashes of Housman, the poet, rest here (tablet on outer N wall).

132 ST. MARY, THIRSK: view from S, showing North Country P massive W tower with many set-offs to buttresses; fretted, pierced and embattled parapet; and fine P windows. It dates from c. 1430, has an earlier-seeming S porch of D design in massive ashlar, and is delicately lighted by its big windows and old tinted glass. The height of the clerestory windows is note-worthy; this differs sharply from West Country churches of about the same date (see Yeovil, 133) which have the typical West Country plan of nave and aisles with separate roofs and no clerestory. In both churches pinnacles are notably absent from the W towers, but parapets run all round tower and church.

133 ST. JOHN THE BAPTIST, YEOVIL: view from S. It shows uniform use of the pure P style, c. 1380-1400, through-out; massive W tower; fine buttresses and parapet to tower, church and S porch; and well-nigh equal-length aisles, nave and chancel, without any clerestory. Like Ludlow (131) this church has transepts and chapels to the E alongside the choir (continuing the line of the aisles); but here there is only a slightly extending chancel, with a D crypt below. The nave arcades have fine, slender cluster-columns; there is a P font; and the famous brass lectern of c. 1450 (see Oundle, 117) is one of five desk-lecterns remaining in England, and the only one in a parish church (the finial to it is later, probably 17C).

134 STS. PETER AND PAUL, LAVENHAM: view from SE, showing rich flint-and-stone flushwork panelling; niches, carvings, etc., in walls, buttresses and parapets of S porch; S (Spring) chapel (1525), and W tower. This is one of the finest examples of late P (1450–85) work in the country. There is still a certain individuality in all this work, but it is yielding to a mechanical accuracy of repetition. The later S windows of the S chapel and aisle show the Tudor style of head; and the ornate complexity of transoms, mouldings, buttresses, parapets, etc., betokens the end of Gothic. The church was built by the Spring family of woolstaplers in collaboration with the 13th Earl of Oxford; the arms of the Springs and De Veres (especially the De Vere mullet, here visible) appear under the tower windows. There is good D work in the older chancel, with finely carved misericords; fine P wooden screens and parcloses contain the chancel and chapels. The ornate S porch was built in 1529 by the 14th Earl of Oxford. The W tower ends abruptly and squarely, without pinnacles. The Spring pew, enclosed by a late screen at the E end of the N aisle, is thought to have been a tomb.

135 STS. PETER AND PAUL, SWAFFHAM: P double hammer-beam chestnut roof, looking W. It shows winged angels on either side of king-posts and at the ends of each hammer-beam. This is reputed to be the finest "angel-roof" in Norfolk, and therefore one of the finest in England. The church dates mainly from 1454. It has inordinately high and long nave and aisles; a small chancel; a fine W tower (1510) with 17C or 18C (see 163) flèche; a deeply recessed W doorway and vast, heavily moulded W window; and a S porch with a simple hammer-beam roof. There are two original P bench-end carvings of the "Swaffham pedlar" and his family (John Chapman, who became rich after having been a pedlar, and rebuilt the N aisle), and of two pedlars with dogs.

136 ST. BOTOLPH, TRUNCH: roof of c. 1500 and top of 16C tabernacle-work font-canopy. The church is late Norfolk D, with P clerestory and roof; there are D nave arcades, a D chancel with a P priests' door and porch, and a fine D W tower. Nave and aisles here form a rectangle without transepts, and the chancel extends as a separate structure. There is good flint-and-stone panelling on the outside; but the treasures are within— the unique single hammer-beam roof open to the roof-frame, with wheels, roses and other carvings in the spandrels; the beautiful screen, matching those at Dennington (105), Bramfield (106) and Southwold (128); and the extraordinary font-enclosure. There are good stalls in the chancel; and the 15C rood-screen shows fine colours, painting, and carving of the diapered grounds of the lower panels. The church is another example of a monumental structure, standing in what was once a thriving community, and is now a village. The Brandons in 1848 gave an excellent ground-plan and lithograph of it in their Parish Churches (see Bibliographical Note, p. 22). See 138.

137 ALL SAINTS, WALSOKEN: Tudor Seven-Sacrament font of 1544, Norman N nave arcade, and Transitional chancel-arch. The defaced font here shows the Crucifixion and Absolution in the upper panels; there are saints in the niches of the pedestal; and the words "Remember the souls of S. Honyter and Margaret his wife, and John Beforth, Chaplain 1544", and emblems, appear round the base. See 47.

138 ST. BOTOLPH, TRUNCH: late 15C font and 16C Tudor canopy. See 136.

139 ST. CYRIAC, LACOCK: late P and Tudor Lady Chapel to N of chancel, showing Renaissance tomb of Sir William Sharington, bold vaulting and pendant groining, ornate arches, and fine carvings. The church has 14C D lower stages to its W tower; 17C battlements, pinnacles and spire to the tower; a D N transept; a rebuilt chancel and S transept of the same period; and a fine P nave (see 152) with a waggon-roof and a cut-away tie-beam at the E end, making room for a fine P window of six lights before the chancel. The porch at the W end was added at the end of the 15C or early in the 16C and has fine vaulting. An odd annexe, once a three-storied and gabled stone house, stands on the W of the S transept; it was probably built in the latter half of the 17C, and now opens into the S aisle.

140 ST. PETER, WINCHCOMB (OR WINCHCOMBE): late 15C or early 16C grotesque on S parapet by S door. This church was begun in 1456 and finished in 1474; the chancel and E ends of the aisles were rebuilt in 1690, and there was drastic restoration in 1872. There are a piscina with two ledges, and remarkable sedilia with saints' niches between the seats. There is some fine old

glass in the S windows, an octagonal font dated 1634, and 40 grotesque gargoyles appear along the clerestory and aisle roofs and parapets. Leland's *Itinerary*, vol. 4, says:

> "In King Henry V tyme, the paroch chyrch of the toune was kept in the body of the monastery. But in King Henry VI tyme one William Winchcombe, abbot, began with the consent of the toune a paroche church at the west end of the abbey . . . and made the east ende of the church. The parishioners had gathered 200*l.* and began the body of the church: but that summe being not able to performe so costly a work, Rafe Boteler, Lord Sudeley, helped them, and finished the worke."

This is an example of relations between clerics and townsfolk, and of an ecclesiastics' choir and laymen's nave.

141 ST. ANDREW, CULLOMPTON: 16C sailors reefing sails, and woolstaplers' crossed shears, on face of buttress of the S Lane chapel. See also 124 and 129. Unfortunately much of this work was "restored" with unsuitable Beer and other stone which—because it was not painted to withstand weather, as medieval stone sculpture generally was—has decayed more rapidly than the original stone.

142 ST. NICHOLAS, BROMHAM: late 15C and early 16C P heraldic stone carvings, gargoyles, etc., of Starky chantry and S aisle parapets and pinnacles. Ashlar work in central tower is also shown. The nave is mainly Norman. The original EE chancel was rebuilt in 1865, retaining its squint and a credence under a trefoil-headed arch. The crossing is EE. The fine Baynton or Beauchamp chapel was built c. 1500 and contains tombs, memorials, etc., of the Baynton, Beauchamp and Starky families.

143 ST. JOHN THE EVANGELIST, CIRENCESTER: W tower of c. 1400, and three-staged S porch of 1500, showing both angle and double lateral buttresses to W tower, flying-buttress (later) from roof of S aisle to SE corner of tower, and various parapets. This is the biggest parish church in Gloucestershire (Tewkesbury is monastic), and is larger than some cathedrals. It has Norman remains on either side of the chancel-arch; Transitional N and S aisles; and re-used Roman material in the S arcade. The E end of the EE chancel

was rebuilt in the 13C, and at the close of that century the S aisle was rebuilt as the chapel of St. John the Baptist. The nave aisles were widened in the 14C; the Trinity chapel on the N side of the N nave aisle was begun in 1430; and St. Katherine's chapel, with its 18C font, dates from 1508. The famous three-staged S porch (here shown), which is the biggest in England and was the meeting-hall of many guilds, was rebuilt in 1836; it was always used for secular purposes as well, and for some time it served as the Town Hall. The Cotswold stone pulpit and font (panelled on bowl and stem) are both good 15C specimens. There is a vaulted crypt beneath the S porch; fine old glass in the W window of the tower, dating from 1430 to 1515 and taken from other parts of the church; and a fine parclose screen to the Garstang chantry of c. 1475. Typical of Cotswold churches, there is a big window with P tracery over the chancel-arch. There is also fan-vaulting in St. Katherine's chapel. The progression towards the late P repetitiveness is noticeable, especially on the tower, where the underlying simple late D or early P style becomes swamped in later panelling.

144 ST. AGNES, CAWSTON: 15C carved and painted rood-screen, from choir looking W, showing hammer-beam roof with angels on beams and winged shields along wall-plate; roof bosses; late D nave arcade; and P clerestory. The angels on the hammer-beams are in feathered "tights" (see also 88 and 128). The church was built by Michael de la Pole, Earl of Suffolk, and his wife at the close of the 14C; the N aisle (shown here) is later P. It is one of the finest in the country, but like so many in East Anglia, it is now the vast church of a small village, and sadly in need of repair. The fine screen depicts, on the W face of the doors and lower panels, the four Doctors of the Church, saints and apostles (St. Matthew has spectacles and a money-box). The figure of the Virgin was taken from the rood and placed for safety on a hammer-beam at the E end of the N side of the nave, nearest the chancel-arch, where it survived the civil War. There is a 14C carved wooden pulpit and an early P (? or late D) font with simple arcading. The W tower is massive, without parapet, spire or pinnacles. There is a bellsolar (or gallery) at the tower-base, on the E face of which is an old English inscription praying God to "spede the Plow" and send barley enough for good ale. Over this gallery probably stood the "plough-rood" which, at the

W end, faced the true rood over the chancel-screen. The church still has "retainers' benches", alongside those of their masters, with lovely poppyheads but (unlike those of their "betters") without any back-rests. See also 154.

145 ST. CATHERINE, LUDHAM: late D chancel of the 14C; early 15C P nave, seen through carved and painted rood-screen (dated 1493) of 12 panels; (rare) royal arms of Elizabeth on W face of tympanum of the boarded-in chancel-arch (for rood on W side, see 150); and hammer-beam nave roof. This church is dedicated to the Saint of Alexandria, whose wheel is the motif used on alternate spandrels over the nave hammer-beams. N and S doors are EE of the 13C; the E window is fine reticulated D; the N porch has good flint flushwork; the S porch is a fine example of the P style; and the P octagonal font (see 150) has symbols of the four evangelists, grotesque beasts below, under them an angel choir, and hirsute male and female "wodehouses" (wodewoses, or wild folk of the woods) on the pedestal. The chancel-roof is thatched, as it was originally. The Elizabethan arms, with the Latin inscription "I am not ashamed of the gospel of Christ—Long live Elizabeth", are noteworthy. St. Apollonia, patron saint of sufferers from toothache, also appears on the W face (the rood) holding a tooth between long forceps. See also Ludlow, 131.

146 ST. MICHAEL AND ALL ANGELS, STANTON HARCOURT: view from SE. It shows the central tower; Norman N nave wall; S transept and S Harcourt chapel wall, windows, buttresses and parapet; EE chancel lancet; and manor-house tower and flag (left of picture). See 83 and 114. It is worth while comparing this view with those (taken from the same angle) of Stoke-sub-Hamdon, 75, and Bredon, 82, both of which admirably show a progression of styles.

147 ST. LEONARD, MIDDLETON (BY MANCHESTER): W tower, built by Cardinal Langley (a native of this place) c. 1430, with (rare) wooden four-gabled cap of 1709. This is a fine historic church amid the reeking chimneys and house-rows of 19C industrialism. The line of Langley's roof can be seen at the W end, inside, below the higher P clerestory and roof of 1524, the date when most of the present church was rebuilt, the nave and N aisle widened, etc. This seems to have been done in gratitude for the English victory over the Scots at Flodden Field.

This church contains the famous "Flodden window", showing Sir Richard Assheton, his wife, chaplain and leading archers—all with long-bow and arrows on their back, and all named in full—kneeling before going off to the battle. See Introduction, p. 16.

148 ST. MARY, TICKHILL: North Country engaged P W tower on D base, with massive-based buttresses, showing fine W windows to aisles and tower, high clerestory, pierced parapets, and mid-wall as well as corner pinnacles. The upper stages of the tower are of c. 1450–1500; the buttresses end with half-engaged pinnacles at the belfry stage; and the "fringe" on the parapet (instead of battlement) is noteworthy. This Yorkshire tower resembles the Somerset kind, and is associated with Walter of Skirlaugh (Yorkshire) who was Bishop of Bath and Wells 1386–8 and brought the design back North with him. This is said to be the finest church in South Yorkshire; it bears on the face of the tower the arms of England with those of Leon and Castile, apparently put there by John of Gaunt 1373–99, who styled himself King of Leon and Castile. The nave is P with a fine clerestory, the N chapel is D, and the lancets of the chancel suggest that it is the original EE structure. The P chancel-arch has an E window above it, as at Lacock, 139, and Cirencester, 143.

149 ST. HELEN, ABINGDON: 15C nave and two 16C parallel aisles on either side, from SW of 16C S aisle. This makes the church five-aisled, and wider than it is long. It has a tower at the NE, which shows EE and D work at the base. The fine D spire, held by flying-buttresses and banded, was rebuilt in 1625 and 1888. It is one of only four stone spires in Berkshire. There are a Jacobean pulpit of 1634 (here visible); a painted wooden ceiling of the 15C; a font-cover of 1636; a chained Bible of 1611; and there are also many fine monuments and memorials to the "merchant princes of Abingdon". The E window and wall of the chancel are modern. The church was originally the rich cloth-working townsmen's answer to the alleged arrogance of "the Abbot of Abbandun" (see Winchcomb, 140).

150 ST. CATHERINE, LUDHAM: P font, nave, clerestory and roof (with St. Catherine's wheels in alternate spandrels above hammer-beams); 15C rood on boarded-in canvas tympanum of chancel-arch, on rood-beam; late 15C screen; and reticulated E window. See 145.

151 ST. NON (OR NONNA), ALTARNUN (ALTARNON): view from SW. It shows Norman or Transitional font of the "Launceston" variety, shaped like cushion-capital, with heads at angles and star or flower on sides; typical Cornish (West Country) triple waggon-roofs, above equal or nearly-equal nave and aisles, without clere-stories; full-width screen (with pieces of modern vault-ing at ends); and carved wooden benches and bench-ends. The church is mainly 15C P; the W tower is late 14C at the base and early 15C at the top stage, 100 ft. from ground, with fine pinnacles; the nave arcades are of granite; the rood-screen is late 15C (only a part of the original remains); and the 79 bench-ends, the finest in Cornwall, are of the same date or early 16C. They include one signed by Robert Daye, their maker, and another of a viol-player. The E window is dated 1534; and the fine row of altar-rails is of 1684.

152 ST. CYRIAC, LACOCK: E end of P N nave arcade, with N transept arch, and (through transept arch) E entrance to Lady chapel with Sir William Sharington's Renaissance tomb. See 139.

153 ST. PETER, WALPOLE ST. PETER: P choir with carved wood and stone stalls, P nave and clerestory with tie-beam roof above, looking W. This church is one of the richest and most imposing of the famous "marshland" wool churches. The third of its kind, it was built 1390-1410, incorporating the late 13C or early 14C D tower with its (later) embattled parapet, which also runs round the nave and chancel. There is a lovely P S porch with two bays, niches, groined ceiling and fine tracery; in it hang a pair of pattens with a notice begging people to take them off at the door—a testi-mony to the marshy land. Beneath the P chancel runs a (rare) subway, to preserve an ancient right of way; this raises the chancel, producing a most impressive effect, viewed either from the nave or from the sanctuary. There is a big Sanctus bellcote above the E gable of the nave, with pinnacled turrets to either side. The noble nave roof is of the 14C, as is that of the N aisle; those of the chancel and S aisle are of the 19C. There is a hand-some Jacobean screen running right across the church E of the S entry; and there are a fine Jacobean pulpit, and oak candelabra. The painted lower part of the rood-screen remains, but is in poor condition. The famous 15C wood-carvings include the wolf holding St. Edmund's head (two arm-rests of choir-stalls), and

poppyheads to low benches in N and S aisles with good linenfold backs. The fine vestry (St. James's chapel) at E end of S aisle has a lovely carved Jacobean oak screen and an iron gate dated 1708. The W door is original D, and those on N and S are late 14C. The fine font, dated 1532, is in a (rare) early 17C unfolding carved wood cover. The Brandons, in their *Parish Churches*, 1848, give splendid lithographs of the Sanctus bellcote and S turret at the E end of the nave, of the N side of the chancel, and of the exterior from both SE and SW, with a ground-plan which includes the subway beneath the altar.

154 ST. AGNES, CAWSTON: view from base of W tower, showing font; "master" pews in centre and backless "retainers'" pews to either side; rood-screen (with door from rood-stair visible above and to left, or N, of screen and chancel-arch); roofs; and remains of painted rood over chancel-arch. See 144.

155 HOLY TRINITY, BLYTHBURGH: W tower and S porch with buttresses and cornice of flint-and-freestone flush-work; unpinnacled buttresses of clerestory; (rare) quatrefoils in circles of parapet; niche of porch with arms below, and Tudor stoup with pedestal beside S door. See 123.

156 ST. SWITHIN, LAUNCELLS: 15C Cornish nave and N aisle, showing granite arcade, carved waggon-roof wall-plates and other timbers to N aisle, some of the 60 typical carved bench-ends (see Altarnun, 151), original tracery of E window to N aisle, and some of the remain-ing Georgian box-pews. There is a Norman font, with double cable-moulding round the bowl; the back of the pew E of the S door contains portions—still coloured—of the vanished rood-screen; the sanctuary floor is made of 1400 15C Barnstaple encaustic tiles, with raised figures and original glaze; and the fine P W tower is of four stages, with battlements and robust pinnacles.

157 ST. MARY, MOLLAND: nave and enclosed post-Reformation chancel, original 16C N aisle, early 18C pulpit and canopy with angel and trump above, 18C box-pews, and characteristic waggon-roofs. It is a typical West Country small church. The nave and chancel are of the 14C; the W tower of the 15C; and the S aisle and its original windows of the late 14C or

early 15C. There is a Transitional font, and there are many lovely wall-memorials and tombs, especially of the Courtenay family (see 200).

158 HOLY TRINITY, TORBRYAN: P waggon-roofed nave and flat-roofed aisles of almost equal length (c. 1400); shallow chancel beyond choir; carved and painted full-width rood-screen of c. 1430; late 17C or early 18C oak box-pews (containing original P and Tudor benches); and Jacobean oak cover to restored font. The remarkable screen, of which the fan-vaulting and loft have disappeared (see Altarnun, 151), remains, with a unique series of painted figures (owing, it is said, to a vigilant rector in Puritan times who covered them with whitewash). These include (rare) St. Victor of Mar-seilles, with a windmill, St. Catherine of Siena, and a figure with a ladder (? St. Emmeran or Alexis). The pulpit (here shown) was made from parts of the rood-screen, and the altar from parts of the original pulpit. The E window is modern.

159 ST. MARY, DENNINGTON: P nave, clerestory, carved benches with poppyheads and box-pews, parclose screen to S chapel, pulpit and lectern in enclosure; and D chancel and E window. See 105 and 119.

160 ST. BOTOLPH, BOSTON: P W tower and D nave and clerestory, from SW. Cox called this "the largest and most impressive parish church in England", and this is true in terms of cubic content, though the church is shorter than some. The high clerestory, parapet, and pinnacled gabled E end of the nave (see Walpole St. Peter, 153), are as impressive from the outside as the splendid P tower with its massive buttresses, flying-buttresses to octagonal lantern at top (see York, 161), and richly varying stages with their long windows and handsome mouldings. The oldest part of the church is the tower-base, begun in 1309. The tower was known as "Boston stump" because it remained unfinished for a long time (completed 1509), the late date of comple-tion accounting for the Tudor effect of the top stage, lantern, etc. It is a landmark for many miles around and out to sea (see Blakeney, 101); the interior is open for 156 ft. as far as the belfry stage, where it is vaulted with an enormous central boss. In the chancel there are 64 stalls with famous carved misericords (school-master teaching, fox preaching to geese, etc.), though the canopies are modern. The monuments and brasses are equally fine.

161 ALL SAINTS PAVEMENT, YORK: view from NE, show-ing equal aisles and nave after destruction of old chancel in 1782; 14C D and 15C P nave, aisles and base of W tower; 15C octagonal lantern (partly later) with 16C and later pinnacles, parapet, etc. The lantern served to light travellers to York through the thick forests which came up to the city gates. Much of the stonework is re-used Roman material from the ancient military capital of Britain, Eboracum. There is much old stained glass, a beautiful sanctuary knocker (rare) on the N door, and a fine P W window.

162 ST. MARY MAGDALENE, LAUNCESTON: Cornish P granite carvings over exterior of equal-length nave, aisles and S porch, from SE. The buttresses of the S porch, walls, pinnacles, etc., and even the E end of the nave are covered with this extraordinary work. It is crude but forceful, and some of it is very effective—e.g. the fine run of buttresses, mouldings, parapet, windows, panelling, and pinnacles along the S aisle wall here. The work is also found outside the now-embodied parish church of St. Mary in Truro cathedral, at Probus (180), and in a few other places in Cornwall. It seems to have been due to the inspiration of a rich wool trader. The P W tower is comparatively narrow and poor for the church. The interior—heavily restored—is remarkable only for the fine arcades with cluster-columns and good capitals.

163 STS. PETER AND PAUL, SWAFFHAM: view from NE, showing high chancel and transepts, Sanctus bellcote over E gable of nave (see Walpole St. Peter, 153), W tower and flèche. See 135.

164 ST. NECTAN, STOKE-BY-HARTLAND: carved and painted rood-screen (c. 1450), from the E, showing vaulting and loft, tie-beam (not rood-beam) above, and painted waggon-roof. The tie-beam had to be inserted in modern times, like the iron tie-rods under the nave roof. The church is mainly D, of the late 14C. The nave arcades are of inordinately wide span. The grand W tower is also a landmark for sailors (compare Blakeney, 101, and Boston, 160); it has poor buttresses, and pinnacles with crosses instead of finials. The Lady chapel roof, painted, gilded and carved, is one of the finest remaining in England. There is a fine West Country late Norman font with square arcaded bowl, and the chancel-floor is noteworthy for its pre-Reforma-tion altar-slabs. The full-width P screen shown here is

one of the best and least restored in the country, but there was another of an earlier period—as can be seen from the pillars on either side.

165 HOLY TRINITY, LONG MELFORD: Clopton family chapel at E end of N aisle looking across altar to tomb S of sanctuary. This private chapel of late P work (1475-1500) has traces of mural paintings; the beams and other timbers (here shown) are painted; verses in Gothic characters by Lydgate, the monk of nearby Bury St. Edmunds, are painted round the cornice (also visible here); and there are noble arcades and canopies, friezes, and (above) niches. The advent of the Tudor style is apparent in all this work. The church itself is a magnificent example of precise and ornate late P work. Beyond its raised chancel, and separated, stands the famous Lady Chapel, also built by the Cloptons (see 172). The W tower is of a later date and has been rebuilt. The fine E window contains most of the remaining old stained glass (including the figure of St. Edmund, King and Martyr), but there is also some in the two W windows. There are many interesting brasses and monuments, and a fine 15C alabaster retable of the Magi. The church is also famous for its remarkable flint-and-stone flushwork; S porch without an upper chamber; parclose screens; and high nave.

166 ST. AUGUSTINE, BROOKLAND: octagonal separate wooden-capped belfry of the 16C, N porch, and nave and chancel roofs. See 43.

167 ST. LAURENCE, BLACKMORE: 15C three-stage wooden W tower and shingled spire, also showing dormer windows of S aisle. The church was the structural nave and aisles of a Norman priory of Austin canons, which extended farther E. In the mid-14C the N arcade (except the W bay) and the N aisle were rebuilt. The W front of the old church is concealed by the wooden W tower, but the W bay shows that the original W end was Norman. The N door in the N porch is 13C, and 14C and 15C doors also remain. The dormers are early Tudor. There is a plain octagonal Purbeck font, said to be Norman but probably 14C D; and at the E end of the S aisle stands the Smyth tomb (modern base) with alabaster effigies of 1594 (see 173).

168 ST. DENYS, STANFORD-IN-THE-VALE: view from W, showing EE W tower (top stage 15C P), EE W window of N aisle, D N porch and window, and Tudor clerestory. The chancel-arch, and probably the N arcade, are EE; but the chancel is D, and most of the church seems to have been rebuilt in the early 14C, when the N porch was added. The S porch is of the 15C (see 188). The nave and clerestory were raised in the 16C. The D chancel contains a beautiful, unique piscina with tabernacle-work over it; there is an extraordinary squint, some old glass, and a (rare) Elizabethan wooden font.

169 ST. ANDREW, SANDON: Tudor red-brick W tower and S porch, and 12C stone, Roman brick and rubble nave. The S walls of the chancel and the SE corner of the nave externally show re-used Roman brick quoins. The chancel-arch was rebuilt, probably late in the 13C; the N arcade and aisle were added mid-14C; and the W tower and S porch are early 16C. There are St. Andrew's crosses in brick on the E and S of the tower; two large Latin crosses on the W; and the three-light W window has fine brick tracery. The brickwork is said to have been carried out for Cardinal Wolsey, who was Lord of the Manor; the two Latin crosses on the W of the tower are said to be his processional crosses. There is a pillar-piscina; a good communion table; and the oldest wine-glass carved pulpit (15C) in Essex.

170 ST. MICHAEL, ASTON UPTHORPE: P W end with Victorian flèche above. This tiny and simple chapel— P aisleless nave and Victorian chancel added—is often confused (as in the Archaeological Institute's 1850 volume on the Diocese of Oxford churches) with Aston Tirrold, which it adjoins. The Upthorpe chapel has a lovely 15C wooden porch on the N.

171 HOLY TRINITY, LITTLEBURY: view from early 16C S porch, looking SE. This is a typical East Anglian flint, rubble and stone porch, and an equally typical churchyard view. See 99.

172 HOLY TRINITY, LONG MELFORD: late P Lady chapel of 1496, from SW. This structure is remarkable within, and almost fantastic (with its flint-and-stone flushwork, geometrical, heraldic, and other patterns) without. It is thought that it was built on so large a scale, and beautified in so many details (e.g. mouldings, shafts and capitals of arcades, niches, engaged shafts at angles, Tudor W doorway with hooded double lights aside,

label and frieze above, fine trussed roofs and wall-plates, etc.) because some valuable holy relics were deposited within the rather obviously "important" central chapel, thus attracting pilgrims. It is certainly out of all proportion to the already big church (see 165).

173 ST. LAURENCE, BLACKMORE: alabaster effigies of Thomas Smyth and his wife Margaret, 1594, on (restored) altar-tomb. He is wearing armour and she a tight dress and ruff. See 167.

174 HOLY TRINITY, BLYTHBURGH: nave arcades, clerestory, aisles and rood-screen, from SW. See 123 and 155. The floor, broken by Cromwell's horsemen, can be seen here.

175 ST. THOMAS, SALISBURY: late P nave, arcades, chancel, roofs, clerestory and chancel-arch, with 16C painted Doom above. The transition to Tudor is everywhere apparent here, save in the remaining D arches at the E ends of the nave aisles (that on the S being shown here). There is also an Annunciation and Salutation painted on the N wall of the Lady chapel. The royal arms of Elizabeth (rare) appear over the S door (see Ludham, 145). This church is a good example of the late P tendency of windows to spread until the walls seem scarcely able to uphold the fabric.

176 ST. OSWALD, LOWER (NETHER) PEOVER: Alderley sandstone W tower of c. 1500, and local half-timbered nave and equal aisles. The church is now mainly of c. 1580, and the interior (see immediately below, 177) shows interesting mixtures of Gothic and Classical motifs—all in wood. Chapels to N and S in the 15C brought the (widened) aisles up square with the chancel at the E end. The roofs are modern, leaving the fine 15C carved beams and trusses in the aisles and nave exposed. There are five octagonal posts aside in the nave; from these run braces for the nave roof tie-beams, braces for the principals on which the nave and aisle roofs rest, and braces for the aisle roof tie-beams (most of these are visible in 177 below). The chancel has much original woodwork; the choir-screen is Jacobean; there is a very old wrought-iron candelabrum in the choir; the 17C altar is 10 ft. 6 in. long; the D (1322) font has a Jacobean wooden cover; and there is a fine inlaid Jacobean pulpit. The box-pews date from 1620 (see 177).

177 ST. OSWALD, LOWER (NETHER) PEOVER: interior from SW. See 176.

178 ST. MARY, EAST GULDEFORD: rectangular nave and chancel combined, of Tudor brick (c. 1505), with 18C twin gabled roof, from SW, showing wooden belfry and 18C buttresses. This church was built by Sir Harry Guldeford after he had secured the saltings of Romney Marsh in 1480, and had reclaimed 1,500 acres by building a sea-wall. It is one of the three old all-brick churches in Sussex. The plaster is vanishing; there is damp on the floors; the structure is weak (see upper NW corner of W face, under roof); and there are no gutters or down-pipes, so the walls are endangered. But it is a strangely imposing building and the interior has a quiet dignity (see 179 below). The structure is of small Tudor bricks, laid in English bond, and a moulded brick string-course surrounds the exterior. The floor is of brick throughout. Even the piscina is of brick (rare).

179 ST. MARY, EAST GULDEFORD: interior, looking W, showing brick floor, 18C box-pews and pulpit, and royal arms of George IV. Note the thickness of the brick walls. See 178.

180 STS. PROBUS AND GRACE, PROBUS: P Cornish granite W tower from NW. It shows rich ornament; eight clusters of foliated pinnacles at the top; elaborate triple buttresses at the corners, ending with pinnacles below parapet; Tudor doorway at the base; and P windows in the upper stages. This tower is one of a few copied from Somerset towers; it is the finest in Cornwall and the highest, was built c. 1550–60, and remains in its original state although the church has been heavily restored. There are a good P E window, some ancient stonework at the altar, and good 16C brasses. The carved work on the outside of the tower is not visible here but resembles that at Launceston, 162, and St. Mary, Truro, near by.

181 ST. MARY, KERSEY: N side of P church and W tower from village ford, showing flint-and-stone flushwork, parapets (unusually high to W tower), single N aisle, nave and chancel. The church has no S aisle, and is really late D, of the late 13C to early 14C. The W tower was completed in 1481. Around 1335 the old N wall of the nave was removed and the present fine N

aisle thrown out, with the intention of building a new nave, and aisles of greater height; but the Black Death in 1348 stopped this, and the Kersey wool trade seems never to have recovered afterwards. There are 15C P porches N and S. That on the S is said to have been built by a fish-wife, of whom a curious carving remains; it is magnificently vaulted, carved, and panelled outside with flint flushwork, which includes its buttresses. There is a fine (restored) D font, and the base of the lectern is 15C P. The church was drastically restored in the last century when the chancel was rebuilt and a new E window was put in. The village gave its name to fabrics known as Kerseys.

182 HOLY TRINITY, TORBRYAN: S porch and door showing later fan-vaulting in earlier P porch, 15C stone bench and steps. See 158.

183 (DEDICATION UNCERTAIN), WHARRAM PERCY: interior of nave, showing Norman arches (nearer) and Transitional arch beyond, with late P windows, and Transitional font. This is the church of what the agrarian enclosures turned into one of England's "lost villages". It was in use as a church until a few years ago, but is rapidly lapsing into ruin (see Introduction, p. 15, and Bibliographical Note, p. 23). There is a good Norman N door, and the S porch has a Transitional door and an early D outer entry. The windows on the N are good D; the extended chancel has an EE arch; and there are many early crosses (down to D) built into the S wall, the S porch, and the vast S buttress to the W tower. The tower is D, above Norman and EE, with P embattled top. See 185.

184 ST. MARY, HADDISCOE: W round flint tower of five stages (upper stage of P embattled flushwork), Transitional and EE coursed stone and flint nave with P windows, and extended P chancel beyond. This is a striking building: the round Saxon W tower is oddly engaged into the W end of the nave, and there is a tall thin Saxon door into it on the E with single-stone imposts, a door or window looking into the nave above; it also has single-splay Saxon lancets and, in its fourth stage, triangular-headed Carolingian double-lights with baluster-shafts between. The single arcade nave (N aisle only) is Transitional and EE with simple piers; the N clerestory (only) is D; and the S windows and

chancel windows are P. There is a fine N wall-painting of St. Christopher and Child (see Hales, 32 and 35), more Byzantine than that at Hales (cf. nimbus and designs on raiment), and a Norman cross on the S wall. The nice P S porch shows good flushwork; inside, over the fine Norman S door, stands an early Norman (? late Saxon) saint in a canopied niche.

185 (DEDICATION UNCERTAIN), WHARRAM PERCY: church and solitary farm cottages from SW, showing vast buttress to W tower, D S porch, late P windows set in Norman arches, rough ashlar coursing of nave in two parts, and the later chancel. See 183.

186 ST. GREGORY, HECKINGHAM: Norman and Transitional nave and apse, thatched, with round contemporary W tower at base (octagonal above), and P S porch. The nave has a lovely EE chancel-arch and N arcade; the E window to the N aisle is D. The W round tower-base is crudely coursed, the upper octagon being of flint with red-brick quoins (shown here). Its lower windows appear to be Saxon. The method of engaging this W tower—octagonal above and round below—in the straight-ended W part of the nave is odd, indicating that the base of the tower (at least) was older than the rest.

187 ST. PETER, CHARNEY BASSETT: view from SE. The church is of many periods, and was attached to the adjoining (ancient) manor. The S wall of the nave (shown here) was part of a Norman 12C building; this was extended W in the 14C; the N aisle was built (? or rebuilt) in the 15C; the chancel was also rebuilt at that time, since the arch is 15C. There are two Norman tympana; that on the S of the chancel is so styled, but it is heavily plastered and probably restored. There is (shown here) a good EE window of two lights S of the chancel, a D window at the W end of the nave, an EE font, and a noteworthy P squint. The screen and pulpit are said to be Jacobean but do not look as old; but the (rare) small rectangular W bellcote is Jacobean or Caroline.

188 ST. DENYS, STANFORD-IN-THE-VALE: 15C P S porch with door and wide buttresses; D window on left (towards W tower), and big late P or early Tudor window of church beyond porch. See 168.

189 ST. MARY, WARWICK: the Lady (or, incorrectly, Beau-champ) chapel. This was begun in 1439, the year of Richard Beauchamp's (Earl of Warwick's) death, in accordance with his testament. It was completed in 1460, consecrated in 1475, and contains (foreground) his tomb of Purbeck marble with effigy of bronze—the making of which involved "imagers", metal-founders, surgeons, and sculptors. A "herse" of five rods covers it: it has 15C untouched enamel bosses; and the bear (of the Warwicks) and griffin (of the Despensers, his second wife's family) appear at the feet. The tomb is surrounded by finely canopied niches for the "weepers" or family friends, with angels between. The tomb of Ambrose Dudley, also Earl of Warwick (created such by Elizabeth, in virtue of his descent from Richard's daughter), lies beyond and to the left of the picture (to S); while to the N (right) lies the ornate Renaissance tomb of Robert Dudley, Earl of Leicester, Elizabeth's favourite, and brother of Ambrose, Earl of Warwick. The chapel, impossible to describe in brief, contains lovely vaulting, fine 15C glass showing saints, etc., a seven-light E window, and, over the W wall, a painting of the Doom carried out by William Bird in 1678 and replacing a former 15C Doom. The stalls are 15C. Up the steps on the right (N) is a small chapel with ex-quisite fan-tracery vault, probably a chantry for Low Mass. The church (see also 197 and 198), built in the early 12C, was collegiate, with secular canons, and is now parish. The Norman crypt remains; chancel, choir and nave were rebuilt by 1394 in the P style; but in 1694 a great fire destroyed much, and the present nave, of c. 1704, with tower, aisles, etc., resulted from the subsequent rebuilding. (The designs of Wren were rejected in favour of those of Sir William Wilson of Sutton Coldfield.) It is a pleasing combination of Gothic and Classical—see 197 and 198—epitomized by Marcus Whiffen (*Stuart and Georgian Churches*, Batsford, London, 1947-8) as both Gothic Survival and Gothic Revival. There is a right of way under the base of the tower (rare—but cf. Walpole St. Peter, 153, where it is at the E end). There are fine statuettes, re-taining much of their original colour, round the E window of the Lady chapel; Gardner attributes these definitely to "imagers". The anatomical detail of the famous Earl's bronze effigy (see above)—which explains the need of a barber surgeon—is exquisite; and the alabaster "weepers'" figures on the earlier tomb of Thomas of Warwick (d. 1371) are splendid examples of the prowess of "imagers" before "sculpture" and "painting" became distinguishable crafts.

190 ST. MARY, CROSCOMBE: late P nave. It shows Jacobean wooden carved screen with royal arms where rood would have been; Jacobean wine-glass pulpit of 1616 and canopy, with pediment like that over arms on screen; and 16C and 17C carved oak box-pews. This big church in a small village, once a rich West Country wool town, is famed for its wealth of woodwork. The screen runs round the E entries to both aisles from the choir; there are also original 15C and 16C oak benches; and the choir contains some fine carved Jacobean stalls. Aisles run almost the entire length of the nave, choir, and chancel, in typical West Country style. There are a fine EE S doorway, a (rare) two-storied vestry, strikingly carved roofs, a noble early P W tower with gargoyles and figures in niches, and fine brasses.

191 ST. MARY, COMPTON WYNIATES (WYNYATES): view of interior, looking SE. This is a Restoration church (1663-6), built after the destruction of the former church (originally private chapel) beside the more famous Tudor manor-house of this same name. It has a rect-angular plan and a central arcade dividing it into two aisles, and it shows both Gothic and Classical motifs pleasantly combined. Arcade, windows, and exterior buttresses are all good P Gothic. The communion-table stands within rails of 1720, on a raised sanctuary against the E arcade pillar (rare). One aisle ceiling was painted with sun and clouds for day, the other with moon and stars for night (a nice reversion to Classicism), but in 1911 the plaster had to be removed, and now only the colourless sun and moon remain on the W wall. The box-pews and pulpit are also of 1720. The marble font (here shown) is Classical. The exterior is Classical, with a tiny W tower and neat cherubs and strap-decoration.

192 ST. PAUL, COVENT GARDEN, LONDON: W front of Tuscan church by Inigo Jones, 1631-3. It has been called the first important Protestant church raised in England (i.e. post-Reformation). It was certainly the only purely Classical church in England in the first half of the 17C. The church today, after the fire of 1795, is a replica of the original built by Jones for the (then) Earl of Bedford's parishioners on his new estate. The Earl is said to have told the architect that he only

needed a barn for them, and to have received the reply, "Then you shall have the handsomest barn in Europe". From his Italian experience, Jones designed an austere Tuscan building, rectangular, aisleless, without chancel —cf. Compton Wyniates immediately preceding—and with a W narthex enclosed within the structure. The Doric E portico juts into the street and is blind, where usually one finds an E window. This was Jones's solution of the problem of an E altar in a rectangular Classical building. He built E porches for side-entrances. It became a parish church in 1645, was restored by Hardwick in 1788 (when Portland stone was used), was gutted in the fire of 1795, and then rebuilt by Hardwick. Butterfield removed the galleries and opened up the interior in 1872, when he restored it. The clock on the E portico was made by Harris in 1641 and is said to be the first with a pendulum in Europe. The exterior is more impressive; the deep Tuscan eaves with their modillions, the pediments and mouldings, all make a fine *chiaroscuro* effect in sunny weather (as here).

193 ST. JOHN THE BAPTIST, BURFORD: the nine sons on one side of the Harman wall-monument (a panel show-ing six daughters is opposed to it); local Renaissance-style stonework of 1569. In a church rich in chapels, chantries, tombs and brasses, etc., this is but one among many monuments (of woolstaplers, etc.)—one of which is the "weeping cherub", in marble, below the memorial to "Kit" Kempster, master-mason to Wren. On the 14C font is scratched "ANTHONY SEDLEY, 1649, PRISNER", the work of one of Cromwell's "Levellers" who were here imprisoned by him for refusing to fight the Irish; three were shot in the churchyard after three days, watched by the rest (including Sedley) from the roof. The magnificent church is a remarkable example of accretions, by the growth of portions of varying styles through the centuries—the ground-plan having by now become well-nigh planless. The N walls alone run true.

194 ST. MARY, BIBURY. 18C Classical tombs, by S porch. See 60.

195 STS. PETER AND PAUL, MUCHELNEY: painted 17C timber waggon-roof with sun-boss. Despite Biblical authority, some of the angels are female and bare-bosomed: a quaint conceit. The colours are red, blue, grey and black, and the sun is quite Classical and

heathen. The church is 15C P, with nave, aisles, and W tower; in the sanctuary there are lovely 13C en-caustic tiles which once made up the floor of the Lady chapel of the adjoining Abbey (in ruins), discovered 4 ft. below the ground. There is also a lovely early D font with carved quatrefoils which may have come from the Abbey.

196 ST. CANDIDA AND HOLY CROSS, WHITECHURCH CANONICORUM: Jacobean Renaissance tomb on N of chancel—a fine example of Italian influence, made exuberant by English fancy in carving and moulding. See 72.

197 ST. MARY, WARWICK: Classical Gothic W tower with passage below, and S aisle, showing P Gothic lines with Classical niches; parapets, urns, etc.; Classical Gothic windows; and Classical P parapet and pinnacles to tower. See 189, also 198 below.

198 ST. MARY, WARWICK: W end of nave and aisles and E arch of tower, showing Classical Gothic piers, columns, capitals, ribs, and window tracery. See 189, also 197 above.

199 ST. ANDREW, BRAMFIELD: The Coke tomb on N chancel wall by Nicholas Stone (1586-1647). Stone received £130 for this. He worked from London and there are examples of his excellent craft in over 100 churches (201, at Croome D'Abitot, is almost cer-tainly his work, as is also the Savage memorial of 1631 at nearby Elmley Castle—these two and this being executed within five years of each other). Both here and at Croome D'Abitot the dead mother holds a chrisom child—one who died before the mother was "churched" and was therefore buried in the (baptismal) chrisom cloth, bound with crossed linen bands. See 102 and 106.

200 ST. MARY, MOLLAND: Classical monuments N of chancel and at E end of N aisle. See 157.

201 ST. MARY MAGDALENE, CROOME D'ABITOT: Classical marble monument of mother and chrisom-child, N of chancel. This monument should be compared with that in 199, by Nicholas Stone. See 209 for description of church.

202 ST. MARY, INGESTRE: interior, looking E. This church was almost certainly (as claimed by the Wren Society) designed by Wren; the evidence is well summarized in Marcus Whiffen's *Stuart and Georgian Churches*, Batsford, London, 1947-8, where the author aptly remarks that "it has a presence beyond its actual dimensions". It was built in three years, finished in 1676, and bears no trace of Gothic within or (if the middle stage of the W tower be excepted) without (see 203). Noteworthy here are the nave cluster-columns raised on bases above the pews; the fine stucco work of the ceilings (coved over the nave, rounded over the chancel); the Classical wooden screen with royal arms above; and the pews conceived as part of the structure.

203 ST. MARY, INGESTRE: W tower, short nave and clerestory, and S aisle. The imposing effect of small parish churches which the peculiar English Classicism of the Wren period achieved, is well shown here. See 202 above.

204 ST. NICHOLAS AND ST. FAITH, ALCESTER: Classical interior (1729-33) of Gothic church. The fine P W tower with traces of D style remains, but chancel, nave and clerestory, arcades, etc., vanished in the 18C remodelling of the interior. The odd effect of the high bases of the nave columns is due to the disappearance of the 18C box-type of high pews and the installation, in 1871, of the low Victorian ones. The disfiguring early 19C galleries were removed in 1871, and the W arch cleared of its organ gallery, thus opening up this startling Classical interior to a Gothic exterior.

205 STS. PETER AND PAUL, LONGBRIDGE DEVERILL: late 17C panelling from Hatfield church, Hertfordshire, behind restored Norman font; fine 20C Classical screen in tower-arch; and one EE arch of S arcade. The church has Norman N, and restored EE S arcades; the W tower is 15C; a N choir aisle forms the Bath chapel of the Thynne family; and there are fine 20C screens of the same Classical design as that shown in the tower-arch here, across the E ends of the aisles.

206 ST. MARY, AVINGTON: unspoiled Classical interior of 1779, with contemporary furnishings. The church is of red brick, typically rectangular and aisleless, without chancel, but with the usual little railed sanctuary, and a fine Classical W tower.

207 ST. LAWRENCE, MEREWORTH: Tuscan nave and W portico, Classical W tower, and copy of spire of St. Martin-in-the-Fields (see 208 below). This spire is a poor copy; the middle stage is truncated; but the *flèche* is pleasantly proportioned, which St. Martin's is no longer. The architect is unknown. The Tuscan exterior and porch—the latter attempting to insert something "spreading" under the tower—are very good, with heavy modillions under equally heavy eaves (cf. St. Paul, Covent Garden, 192, and Gibbs's smaller but similar attempt under his St. Mary-le-Strand W tower, 221). This problem—a peculiarly English one, which Inigo Jones evaded at St. Paul, Covent Garden, by omitting a tower altogether—always arises in a combination of W towers with the Classical style. The interior here (see 210) is Doric (see Stoke Edith, 211), with barrel vault to nave, flat ceilings to aisles, and a nice repeated colonnade round the walls. The whole creates an Egyptian as well as a Greek-Italian effect.

208 ST. MARTIN-IN-THE-FIELDS, LONDON: W front and steeple from portico of National Gallery. This was perhaps Gibbs's finest work (1722-6), with an absolutely Classical exterior and W portico (shown here, with royal arms in the tympanum) and the tower engaged in the nave beyond: a happier solution of the problem posed by a W tower and Classical rectangular design than he had achieved some five years earlier at St. Mary-le-Strand (221).

209 ST. MARY MAGDALENE, CROOME D'ABITOT: Gothic Revival (1761-3) chancel, N aisle, ogee chancel-arch, and moulded plaster crockets and other motifs on chancel-arch, roofs, cornices, etc. The church was built, by an unknown architect, for the Earl of Coventry, the tombs of whose family, including that shown in 201, crowd the chancel and the underlying vault. It contains a remarkable collection of English monumental sculpture. The one shown in 201 (extreme E, on right) has a fine Baroque canopy with typical broken pediment, serpentine pillars, etc. Sculpture, lettering, decoration, etc., are of outstanding quality. Like Ingestre (202-3), Mereworth (207, 210), and many others of this period, this church is an example of the rich lords' revived patronage of both ecclesiastical and secular arts.

210 ST. LAWRENCE, MEREWORTH: S aisle showing 18C marble pedestal font (see also 213), Doric S wall-colonnade, and flat ceilings to aisle bays. The church originally had no pews; these are of the 19C. The older tombs in the W private chapel are of the Fanes and Despensers.

211 ST. MARY, STOKE EDITH: 15C P base of W tower and angle-buttresses; later (? 16C) octagonal solid stone panelled spire on arched squinches; Classical (1740) nave. The nave is a plain rectangular hall, with Doric columns (see Mereworth, 210) across the sanctuary at the E end, and a W gallery. There is a quaint Classical marble font-bowl on a wrought-iron pedestal-frame, and a fine (? 15C) tomb-slab of a lady under the gallery opposite the S door.

212 ST. PETER, WALLINGFORD: Gothic Revival W tower and spire (1777) by Sir Robert Taylor, inspired by Wren's Renaissance spire of the now-ruined St. Bride's, Fleet Street, London. Noteworthy are the cinquefoil-headed lights of the octagonal lantern, and the pierced and banded spire with its metal-work effect. The church (1769) is not by Taylor; it was restored and refurnished in the last century. The chancel was added in 1904. Lawyers will note that this elegant spire was erected at the cost of Blackstone.

213 ST. MARY MAGDALENE, CROOME D'ABITOT: pure Renaissance font (c. 1763) at W end of nave, showing early Gothic Revival W door beyond. See 201, 209 and 215.

214 STS. PETER AND PAUL, TEIGNGRACE: nave, looking W, of the "Strawberry Hill Gothic" brick and stone church, built in 1787 by the Temple family of nearby Storer House (1776). The style is debased EE with much Victorian restoration. The church has a nave, small embattled apse, transepts half-way up the nave, and a W porch with tower above. There is a fine and effective copy of a Vandyke *Pietà* by Sir James Barry, R.A.

215 ST. MARY MAGDALENE, CROOME D'ABITOT: Gothic Revival exterior from SW, in the park (by "Capability" Brown) of Croome Court. The church, on the highest ground and against trees, shows a delightful mingling of the traditional Gothic with Classical severity. Noteworthy here are the fine arches at the base of the W tower (two blind), bold quatrefoils above (and below parapet), niche in W wall of S aisle, and heavy embattled parapet of nave and aisle. See 201, 209 and 213.

216 ST. JOHN THE EVANGELIST, SHOBDON: Rococo Gothic interior, built by an unknown architect for the second Viscount Bateman, 1753: "wedding-cake Gothic" might be an apter phrase for this charming red-white-and-blue fantasy, with ogee arches, pendants, cluster-columns, and plaster cornices and decorations. The W gallery (shown here) was nicely added in 1810. The church is exquisitely proportioned throughout, with shallow transepts forming pews for the Batemans (S) and their retainers (N), and shallow chancel (from which the picture is taken). Lord Bateman pulled down the lovely Norman church (except for the 14C W tower, which remains here) and placed the fine Kilpeck-like carved arches, columns, etc. (36 and 40) farther N in the park. The non-functional (and therefore Rococo and un-Gothic) triple ogee arches, with two pendants over chancel and transepts (shown here), are unique. The effect is that of a rich man's tasteful whim. The font (also shown) is Norman, of 1165, with beasts round the base.

217 STS. PETER AND PAUL, CHERRY WILLINGHAM: Classical rectangular church, lantern and cupola (c. 1753, the same date as Shobdon, 216) from NW. It has a simple nave with small E apsidal chancel, flat painted roof, no galleries, three large Classical round-headed windows aside, and no W windows.

218 STS. PETER AND PAUL, BLANDFORD: Classical church, W tower, lantern and cupola, from SW. The famous Bastard brothers, natives of the town, built this imposing church after the fire which destroyed most of the town in 1731. It has an apsidal choir and chancel, with both choir and chancel arches; shallow but high nave porches N and S (shown here); Ionic nave colonnades; fine 18C box-pews; and a charming W minstrels' gallery, supported on fluted wooden columns, with a bowed front. The later side-galleries spoil the nave colonnades and cut the windows half-way.

219 GROSVENOR CHAPEL, SOUTH AUDLEY STREET, LONDON: W front of Classical brick chapel built in 1730 on the expanding Grosvenor estate as a dependency of St. George's, Hanover Square, by an unknown

architect. The original and similar spire rose from a plain square W tower; but in 1800 the present intermediate stage was introduced and the spire faced with Roman cement. In 1951 this was restored, the spire painted blue and the doors red. Without the W tower and spire this church looks like a theatre. Inside, the architect has solved the 18C gallery problem by running the gallery right round the church on piers, with round columns from it to support the roof, and by inserting two tiers of windows all round. Lady Mary Wortley Montagu, who introduced inoculation for smallpox by trying it on her children, was buried here in 1762, and there is a tablet to John Wilkes, "a Friend to Liberty" (1797); but it is likely to become better known as the church where Gen. Eisenhower's European Headquarters' staff worshipped between 1942 and 1945, and rendered thanks for victory.

220 ST. JOHN THE BAPTIST, KNUTSFORD: Classical W tower of red brick with stone quoins, and S aisle with S door, stone dressings of windows, parapet, etc. This brick church was built in 1744 and has extended aisles and nave far too long for its proportions. There is a fine contemporary two-tier candelabrum inside.

221 ST. MARY-LE-STRAND AND ST. CLEMENT DANES, LONDON: view from W. St. Mary-le-Strand was the first of the 50 new churches ordered to be built in Queen Anne's reign, of which Wren (one of the Commissioners) wrote:

"It would be vain to make a parish church larger than that all who are present can both hear and see. The Romanists, indeed, may build larger churches; it is enough if they hear the murmur of the Mass, and see the Elevation of the Host; but ours are to be fitted for auditories."

This was in keeping with the recent Protestant Succession, with whose requirements many short, compact, Classical churches in England are also in accord. Gibbs designed this church without a W tower, intending it to be flanked by a 250 ft. high column (twice the height of Nelson's column) crowned by a statue of the Queen. She died before this plan could be executed, and the church was finished (c. 1717) with its tower and steeple rising from the nave roof, and semicircular W portico beneath (see Mereworth, 207). It is more experimental than St. Martin-in-the-Fields (208) but

not as harmonious a whole, being too narrow and high for its steeple. Beyond, are the W tower and spire of the famous church of St. Clement Danes, built in 1682, by Pierce, to Wren's plans. The spire was added by Gibbs in 1719. Only the tower and shell survived the bombing of London.

222 ST. JAMES, PENTONVILLE, LONDON: W front of "Regency" chapel, c. 1790 (now church) by Thomas Hardwick, showing stucco pilasters, fanned arches, niches and other Regency motifs against black brick structure. There is no more charming example of a late Classical church than this, though it seems more like a theatre or town hall (cf. also 219, half a century earlier, and then the early 19C Gothic Revival style of 223 which could be nothing but a church). Few who pass this little church know that Grimaldi, the clown, and Bonington, the "boy genius" painter claimed both by France and England, are buried there.

223 ST. PETER, BRIGHTON: Gothic Revival S front and tower, 1823-8, by Sir Charles Barry. The church had a polygonal apse and galleries, now removed. It shows Barry's earlier and more sensitive Gothic work, but he was not permitted to build one of the Gothic spires which he deemed essential to true Gothic. (As Whiffen says, however, this was all to the good.) The church was designed to finish off the N end of the famous Steyne, which led Barry to make as wide and heavy a base as possible, with vast pinnacled buttresses, screen walls, flying-buttresses to the tower-corners, and a door (and window above) inside the big S arch and its canopied frame.

224 ST. MARY, BEDFORD: Gothic Revival S arcade and aisle (1853); part of older S wall left as buttress to Norman tower; Norman crossing; Gothic Revival N arcade (1840); 14C chancel; and restored and whitewashed interior, with 19C pews, and modern lighting. This is an example of what imagination can do to an old and composite church; it is now light and cheerful. Of the old church remain the Norman crossing, transepts, central tower and W wall; the 14C chancel window jambs, sedilia, piscina, and "low side-window" (restored); the 15C upper stage and parapet of central Norman tower; and the 16C N aisle and windows. As in many old churches, the tower, nave, chancel, and aisle walls are misaligned.

225 ST. JAMES, HARTLEBURY: Gothic Revival church, 1836–7, by Thomas Rickman, showing slender cluster-columns, plaster vaults, and Rickman's solution of the gallery problem (see Blandford, 218). Galleries run behind the nave arcades and well within the aisles. At this date, when Victoria became Queen, the Gothic was about to win a victory both "crushing and complete"; the Classical (with its Baroque and Rococo offspring) was finished. Here—though not his best work—Rickman was experimenting, but was holding more tightly to the dictates of "pure" Gothic. Part of the chancel is early 14C, and the W tower bears the date 1587.

226 ST. SWITHUN, WICKHAM: Benjamin Ferrey's early Victorian Gothic nave of 1845–9. He also rebuilt the aisles and chancel. The nave arcades were copied from the fine D arcade at Stoke Golding, Leicestershire. The angels on the hammer-beams are *papier-mâché*; there are elephants' heads of the same material on those of the N aisle (said to be from the 1862 Paris Exhibition). Belgian and English gaily-coloured glass abounds; the W tower-arch into nave (here shown) has fine tracery; but the niches on either side, and both the font in front and its cover (carved in New Zealand, but not by Maoris, as is often said) can only be termed "improbable" Gothic. The church is of rubble and fine coursed and knapped flint in East Anglian fashion—rare in Berkshire—with stone quoins. A small Roman pillar divides a double-light window in the lovely Saxon W tower, which has "long-and-short" work and one other Saxon window on its W face. The tower is so thick that it has been described as defensive; there is a room in the middle stage, and no trace of a door at the base. The story of the English parish churches is aptly epitomized in the combination here of early Saxon work with "Albert Memorial" Gothic, separated by more than a millennium of English history.

The styles in English architecture do not fall into hard and fast periods, agreed by all authorities, but the following will serve as a guide to the approximate dates of the principal phases:

Saxon	7C to 1050
Norman	1050 to 1190
Transitional	1150 to 1200
Early English	1190 to 1250
Decorated	1250 to 1350
Perpendicular	1300 to 1550
Tudor	1500 to 1600
Renaissance, Jacobean, Caroline, Stuart, etc.	1575 to 1700
Classical	1600 to 1830
Gothic Revival	1750 onwards

It must be remembered, however, that there was considerable overlapping of styles between these periods and that at some stages—particularly between 1550 and 1750—many different styles persisted simultaneously. It should further be remembered that the Gothic style was always to a greater or less extent in evidence; when, therefore, the term "Gothic Revival" is used, the special characteristics associated with the revival of the Gothic style after 1750 are referred to.

GLOSSARY

ABACUS: A slab at the top of a capital, like a cap or crown over it.

AISLE: Literally "wing"; the sideway extension of the nave.

APSE: Rounded or polygonal end—generally eastern—of a church, transept, or chapel.

ASHLAR: Masonry or squared stones in regular courses.

BAY: Compartment(s) dividing the nave or roof of a building. Also a projecting window.

BUTTRESS: Masonry built against a wall to strengthen it, or to resist the outward thrust of an arch or vault from above. (See FLYING-BUTTRESS.)

CAPITAL: Topmost portion of a column or pier, or of a whole group of columns and piers.

CHANCEL: The holy place where the altar is situated, behind the "bar" or rails.

CHANTRY: Place (e.g. chapel) where prayers were to be said for the soul of the founder(s) who had left a fund for that purpose.

CHOIR: Part of church for the use of singers, generally between nave and chancel and separated from the nave by rail or screen.

CLERESTORY: Upper part of nave wall, containing windows, generally above the aisle roofs.

CLUNCH: A soft, white limestone.

COPING: The capping or covering along the top of a wall.

CORBEL: A bracket, often elaborately carved or moulded, projecting from a wall to support the beams of a roof, the ribs of a vault, or a statue.

CORNICE: A projection round or along the top of buildings or rooms. In Classical or Renaissance buildings, it is the upper part of the entablature.

COURSE: A continuous line of stones, bricks, etc., evenly laid along a wall.

CROCKET: A projecting knob of a stone, carved with curving foliage, arranged in sequence along the lines of spires, canopies of tombs, gables, etc.

CROSSING: Intersection of the nave of a church with the transepts, sometimes supporting a (central) tower.

CRYPT: Literally "secret" place; originally the underground chamber where a martyr's, then a saint's, relics rested beneath the high altar; later, any underground chamber below a church, e.g. a charnel or bone-house.

CUSP(S): The projecting points formed by the intersection of the small arcs or foils in tracery.

DRIP-COURSE: A projecting course to catch and throw off rainwater. (See WATER-TABLE.)

ENGAGED: Attached to the fabric, e.g. a pilaster.

ENTABLATURE: The entire horizontal portion resting on the columns in Classical architecture.

FOIL: Small opening, or curved "bite", taken out of the stone or wooden members of door and window openings, or of decorative arcading. According to their grouping in threes, fours, fives, etc., they are known as trefoil, quatrefoil, cinquefoil, etc.

FLUSHWORK: Inlaid stone and flush-faced flint work, in patterns, found mainly in East Anglian flint districts.

FLYING-BUTTRESS: An external arch springing over the roof of an aisle and supporting the wall of the clerestory. It is also used to support the sides of spires and lanterns, and is sometimes called an arch-buttress.

FRIEZE: The middle part of the entablature in Classical architecture.

GABLE: Triangular portion of a wall between the enclosing lines of a sloping roof.

HAMMER-BEAM: A projecting beam to support a roof by "building-up", i.e. without a direct tie-beam across.

IMPOST: Upper portion of a pier, column or pillar, usually moulded, on which an arch rests.

JAMB: The upright side-member of a door, window, etc.

KEYSTONE: The central and topmost voussoir, locking the arch. (See VOUSSOIR.)

KING-POST: Central member of a roof-truss, extending from the ridge or apex of the roof to the tie-beam, on which it apparently rests but which it supports.

LIGHT(S): Distinct openings of mullioned and transomed windows.

LINTEL: The horizontal member across the top of a door.

MISERICORD: Tip-up seat in choir-stalls, having a smaller support on the underside, frequently grotesquely carved, on which the user might recline yet remain, technically, "on his feet".

MODILLION: A bracket, or projecting member, to support the upper members of a cornice.

MOULDING: Contours given to any projections, generally by carving.

MULLION(S): Vertical member(s) of a window, dividing it into a number of lights.

NARTHEX: An extrance-annex before the main portal, generally in early churches, and at the west end.

NAVE: From Latin *navis*, a ship; the western and main body of the church, for ordinary folk.

PIER: A mass of masonry (as distinct from a pillar or column) from which an arch springs. Sometimes applied to the portions of a wall between doors and windows.

PILASTER: A pillar attached to (engaged in) the wall and projecting only about one-sixth of its breadth from the wall.

PISCINA: Literally "fishpond"; a washing-and-draining stoup in a niche near the altar, generally let into the wall, for cleansing sacred vessels.

POPPYHEAD: Head of a bench, or pew-end, brought up to a carved figure or emblem.

PRESBYTERY: Eastern part of a large church, kept exclusively for the use of clergy; applied sometimes to the choir only, but often to the whole sanctuary.

QUOIN(S): Corner-stone(s) at the angles of buildings; sometimes applied to the angle itself.

REREDOS: Decorative long panel above, and sometimes all round, an altar.

ROOD: Crucifix; generally the one which stood upon the screen separating chancel from nave before the Reformation, but also applied to one found (as in Saxon times) on the outside of a church or on a standing cross.

ROUNDEL: A moulded opening or niche of circular form.

RUBBLE: Uncut stone of all shapes and sizes, laid at random without courses.

SCREEN: A generally elaborate barrier or division between portions of the church reserved for special purposes, e.g. between nave and choir or chancel (see ROOD above), or between chantries or other chapels and nave, choir, chancel, transepts, or aisles.

SCREEN WALL: A wall carried up above the line of vision, but not to the ceiling.

SEDILIA: Seats for priests, generally cut out of the south wall by the main altar.

SHAFT: Portion of a column between base and capital; also a small column supporting a vaulting rib.

SOFFIT: The ceiling, or underside, of any architectural member, e.g. of an arch.

SPANDREL: Space between the head of any arch (or door, window, etc.) and the frame in which it is set; also the space left between two adjoining arches.

SPLAY: Diagonal surface formed by the cutting away of the wall round a door or window; the opening then becomes wider inside than outside, or *vice versa*; hence "splayed inwards" or "outwards".

SPRINGER: The lowest stone of an arch, rib, or vault, at the point where the arch begins to "spring".

STRING-COURSE: A projecting band of stones, or moulding, along a wall.

TRACERY: Ornamental pattern(s) formed by the tracing, or interweaving, of the mullions in the head of a window; applied also to similar work in wood screens and panelling.

TRANSEPT: That part of a cruciform church which projects at right angles to the main building, usually to north and south, forming the arms of a cross; sometimes called a cross-aisle.

TRANSOM: Horizontal member of a window; the cross-bar.

TRIFORIUM: The middle space between the clerestory above, and the nave-piers and aisles below; it often forms a gallery or passage above the roofs of the aisles and, having no windows to the open air, is sometimes called a "blind-story".

TRIGLYPH: Blocks, cut with three vertical channels, placed at regular intervals along the frieze of the Doric style of entablature.

TRUSS: A framed support for a roof, standing vertically, and dividing the roof into bays.

TYMPANUM: Semicircular or semioval slab, filling up the space between the lintel and arch of a door; generally (but not always) Saxon or Norman, since their doors were mainly set in rounded portals.

VAULT: An arched roof built with stone or brick.

VOUSSOIRS: Stones in an arch or vault, so trimmed that their sides taper towards the imaginary centre of the circle of that arch; thus the more pressure falls upon them, the more tightly they hold together.

WATER-TABLE: Like a drip-course, a moulding or projection to catch and throw off rain or water.

1. BRADFORD-ON-AVON, Wiltshire

2. BRADFORD-ON-AVON, Wiltshire

3. ESCOMB, Durham

4. WORTH, Sussex

5. BREAMORE, Hampshire

6. HADSTOCK, Essex

7. TUNSTALL, Lancashire

8. KIRKBY STEPHEN, Westmorland

9. BRITFORD, Wiltshire

10. HEYSHAM, Lancashire

11. INGLESHAM, Wiltshire

12. BARNACK, Northamptonshire

13. MIDDLETON-BY-PICKERING, Yorkshire

14. BRIXWORTH, Northamptonshire

15. LANGFORD, Oxfordshire

16. **SOMPTING**, Sussex

17. BARNACK, Northamptonshire

18. CAMBRIDGE

19. BRIXWORTH, Northamptonshire

20. WORTH, Sussex

21. EARLS BARTON, Northamptonshire

22. STAPLEHURST, Kent

23. WING, Buckinghamshire

24. COLCHESTER, Essex

25. BISHOPSTONE, Sussex

26. CHICKNEY, Essex

27. AVEBURY, Wiltshire

28. MELBOURNE, Derbyshire

29. SOMPTING, Sussex

30. SOMPTING, Sussex

31. IFFLEY, Oxfordshire

32. HALES, Norfolk

33. STOW, Lincolnshire

34. IFFLEY, Oxfordshire

35. HALES, Norfolk

36. KILPECK, Herefordshire

37. BARFREYSTONE, Kent

38. BARFREYSTONE, Kent

39. BARFREYSTONE, Kent

40. KILPECK, Herefordshire

41. GREAT CANFIELD, Essex

42. ROCHE, Cornwall

43. BROOKLAND, Kent

44. NORTHAMPTON

45. AVEBURY, Wiltshire

46. MELBOURNE, Derbyshire

47. WALSOKEN, Norfolk

48. PATRIXBOURNE, Kent

49. CAMBRIDGE

50. OLD SHOREHAM, Sussex

51. NEW SHOREHAM, Sussex

52. STEWKLEY, Buckinghamshire

53. NEW SHOREHAM, Sussex

54. CASSINGTON, Oxfordshire

55. CHALDON, Surrey

56. OLD SHOREHAM, Sussex

57. LONDON

58. LONDON

59. NEW SHOREHAM, Sussex

60. BIBURY, Gloucestershire

61. BLEWBURY, Berkshire

62. WEST WALTON, Norfolk

63. BREDON, Worcestershire

64. UFFINGTON, Berkshire

65. INGLESHAM, Wiltshire

66. NEW ROMNEY, Kent

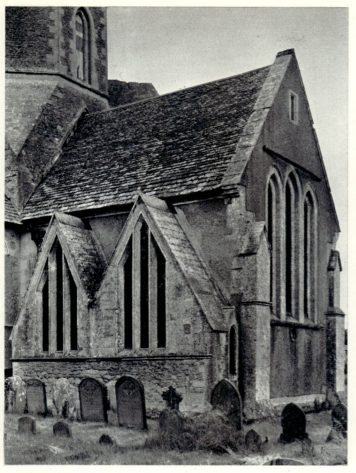

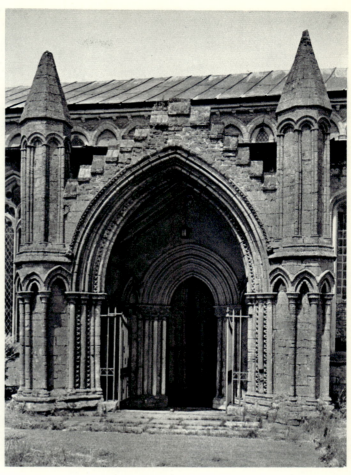

67. UFFINGTON, Berkshire

68. WEST WALTON, Norfolk

69. LANGFORD, Oxfordshire

70. INGLESHAM, Wiltshire

71. **DORCHESTER**, Oxfordshire

72. WHITECHURCH CANONICORUM, Dorsetshire

73. WEST WALTON, Norfolk

74. EDINGTON, Wiltshire

75. STOKE-SUB-HAMDON, Somersetshire

76. ARLINGTON, Sussex

77. OTTERY ST. MARY, Devonshire

78. BERE REGIS, Dorsetshire

79. WEST WALTON, Norfolk

80. KETTON, Rutland

81. **POLEBROOK**, Northamptonshire

82. BREDON, Worcestershire

83. STANTON HARCOURT, Oxfordshire

84. FARINGDON, Berkshire

85. DROITWICH, Worcestershire

86. FARINGDON, Berkshire

87. EAST HAGBOURNE, Berkshire

88. SALLE, Norfolk

89. BAMPTON, Oxfordshire

90. ASHWELL, Hertfordshire

91. COATES-BY-STOW, Lincolnshire

92. COATES-BY-STOW, Lincolnshire

93. BAULKING, Berkshire

94. BUGTHORPE, Yorkshire

95. NORTH HINKSEY, Berkshire

96. BESSELSLEIGH, Berkshire

97. CLEY, Norfolk

98. CLEY, Norfolk

99. LITTLEBURY, Essex

100. SUTTON COURTENAY, Berkshire

101. BLAKENEY, Norfolk

102. BRAMFIELD, Suffolk

103. TUNSTALL, Lancashire

104. GREAT SALKELD, Cumberland

105. DENNINGTON, Suffolk

106. BRAMFIELD, Suffolk

107. LECHLADE, Gloucestershire

108. MARKET HARBOROUGH, Leicestershire

109. WINCHELSEA, Sussex

110. LOUTH, Lincolnshire

111. MORWENSTOW, Cornwall

112. MARNHULL, Dorsetshire

113. HADSTOCK, Essex

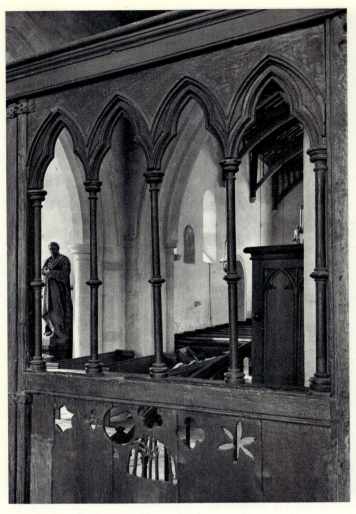

114. STANTON HARCOURT, Oxfordshire

115. MARCH, Cambridgeshire

116. BALSHAM, Cambridgeshire

117. OUNDLE, Northamptonshire

118. **PICKERING**, Yorkshire

119. **DENNINGTON**, Suffolk

120. WORSTEAD, Norfolk

121. HUISH EPISCOPI, Somerset

122. MARTOCK, Somerset

123. BLYTHBURGH, Suffolk

124. CULLOMPTON, Devonshire

125. SAFFRON WALDEN, Essex

126. THAXTED, Essex

127. TIVERTON, Devonshire

128. SOUTHWOLD, Suffolk

129. CULLOMPTON, Devonshire

130. LOUTH, Lincolnshire

131. LUDLOW, Shropshire

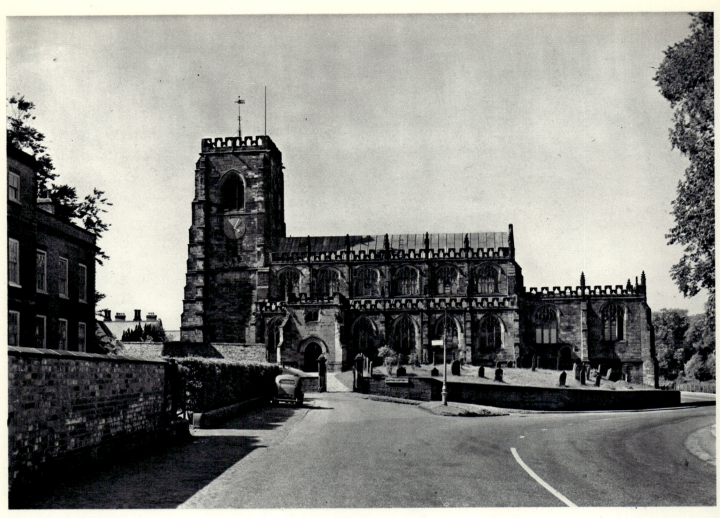

132. THIRSK, Yorkshire

133. YEOVIL, Somersetshire

134. LAVENHAM, Suffolk

135. SWAFFHAM, Norfolk

136. TRUNCH, Norfolk

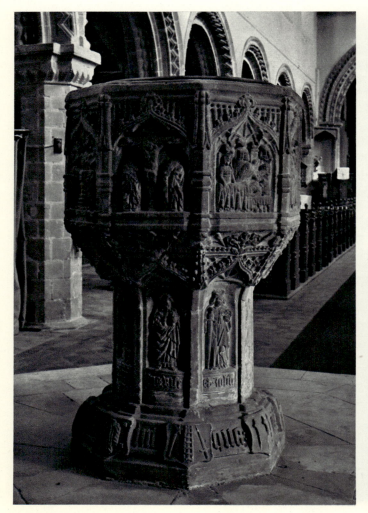

137. WALSOKEN, Norfolk

138. TRUNCH, Norfolk

139. LACOCK, Wiltshire

140. WINCHCOMB, Gloucestershire

141. CULLOMPTON, Devonshire

142. BROMHAM, Wiltshire

143. CIRENCESTER, Gloucestershire

144. CAWSTON, Norfolk

145. LUDHAM, Norfolk

146. STANTON HARCOURT, Oxfordshire

147. MIDDLETON (BY MANCHESTER), Lancashire

148. TICKHILL, Yorkshire

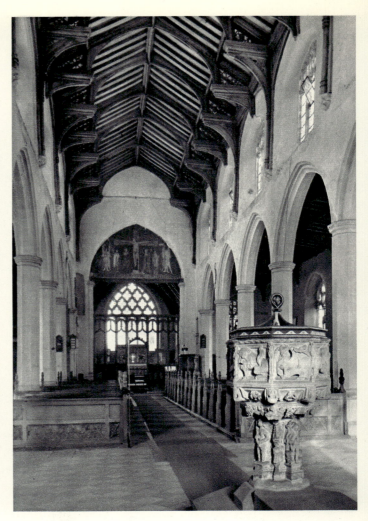

149. ABINGDON, Berkshire

150. LUDHAM, Norfolk

151. ALTARNUN, Cornwall

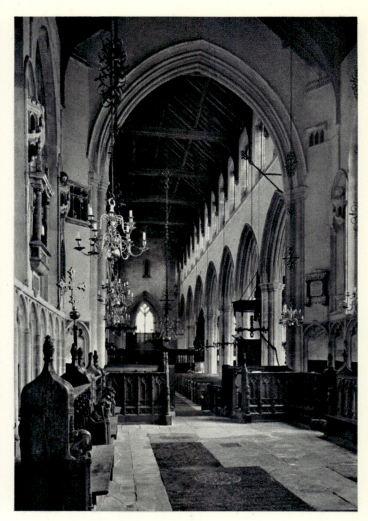

152. LACOCK, Wiltshire

153. WALPOLE ST. PETER, Norfolk

154. CAWSTON, Norfolk

155. BLYTHBURGH, Suffolk

156. LAUNCELLS, Cornwall

157. MOLLAND, Devonshire

158. TORBRYAN, Devonshire

159. DENNINGTON, Suffolk

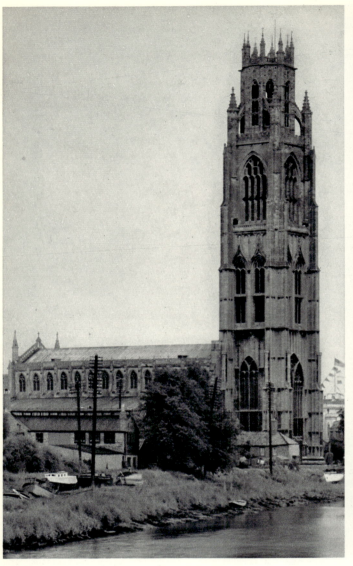

160. BOSTON, Lincolnshire

161. YORK

162. LAUNCESTON, Cornwall

163. SWAFFHAM, Norfolk

164. STOKE-BY-HARTLAND, Devonshire

165. LONG MELFORD, Suffolk

166. BROOKLAND, Kent

167. BLACKMORE, Essex

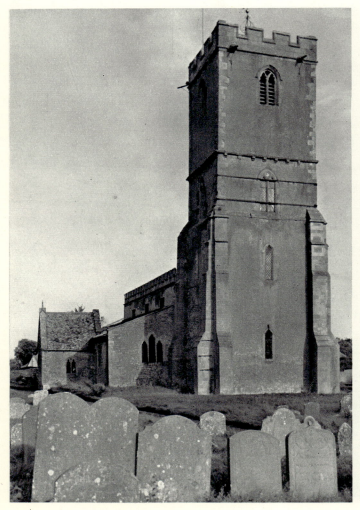

168. STANFORD-IN-THE-VALE, Berkshire

169. SANDON, Essex

170. ASTON UPTHORPE, Berkshire

171. LITTLEBURY, Essex

172. **LONG MELFORD**, Suffolk

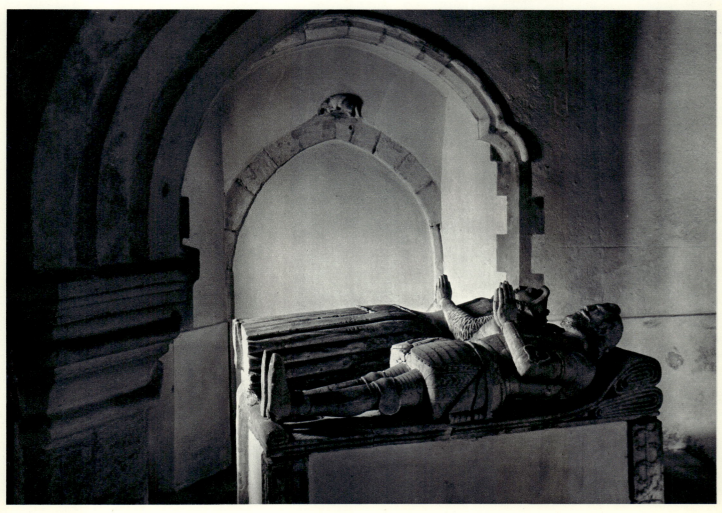

173. **BLACKMORE**, Essex

174. BLYTHBURGH, Suffolk

175. SALISBURY, Wiltshire

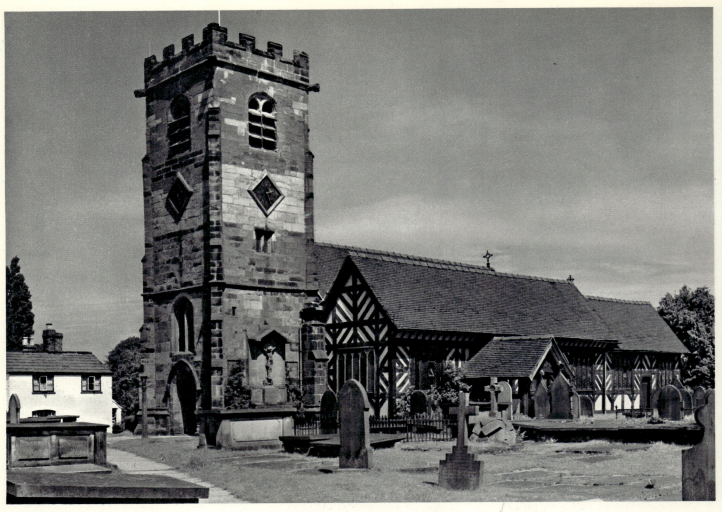

176. **LOWER PEOVER**, Cheshire

177. **LOWER PEOVER**, Cheshire

178. EAST GULDEFORD, Sussex

179. EAST GULDEFORD, Sussex

180. PROBUS, Cornwall

181. KERSEY, Suffolk

182. TORBRYAN, Devonshire

183. WHARRAM PERCY, Yorkshire

184. HADDISCOE, Norfolk

185. WHARRAM PERCY, Yorkshire

186. **HECKINGHAM,** Norfolk

187. **CHARNEY BASSETT,** Berkshire

188. STANFORD-IN-THE-VALE, Berkshire

189. WARWICK

190. CROSCOMBE, Somersetshire

191. COMPTON WYNIATES, Warwickshire

192. LONDON

193. BURFORD, Oxfordshire

194. BIBURY, Gloucestershire

195. MUCHELNEY, Somersetshire

196. WHITECHURCH CANONICORUM, Dorsetshire

197. WARWICK

198. WARWICK

199. BRAMFIELD, Suffolk

200. MOLLAND, Devonshire

201. CROOME D'ABITOT, Worcestershire

202. INGESTRE, Staffordshire

203. INGESTRE, Staffordshire

204. ALCESTER, Warwickshire

205. LONGBRIDGE DEVERILL, Wiltshire

206. AVINGTON, Hampshire

207. MEREWORTH, Kent

208. LONDON

209. CROOME D'ABITOT, Worcestershire

210. MEREWORTH, Kent

211. STOKE EDITH, Herefordshire

212. WALLINGFORD, Berkshire

213. CROOME D'ABITOT, Worcestershire

214. TEIGNGRACE, Devonshire

215. CROOME D'ABITOT, Worcestershire

216. SHOBDON, Herefordshire

217. CHERRY WILLINGHAM, Lincolnshire

218. BLANDFORD, Dorsetshire

219. LONDON

220. KNUTSFORD, Cheshire

221. LONDON

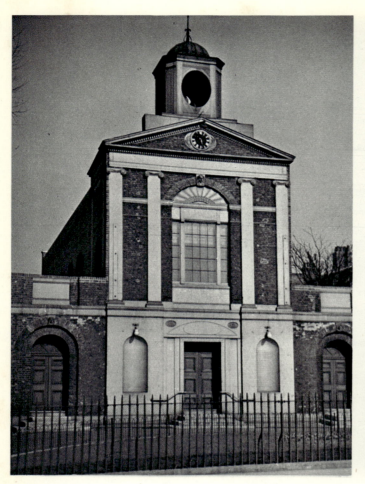

222. LONDON

223. BRIGHTON, Sussex

224. BEDFORD

225. HARTLEBURY, Worcestershire

226. WICKHAM, Berkshire

CHURCHES APPEARING IN THIS BOOK

The numbers are identical with those of the Plates and the corresponding Notes. Only the first reference is marked on the map

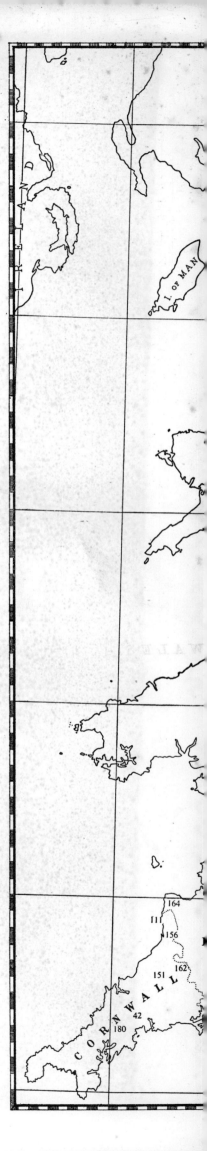

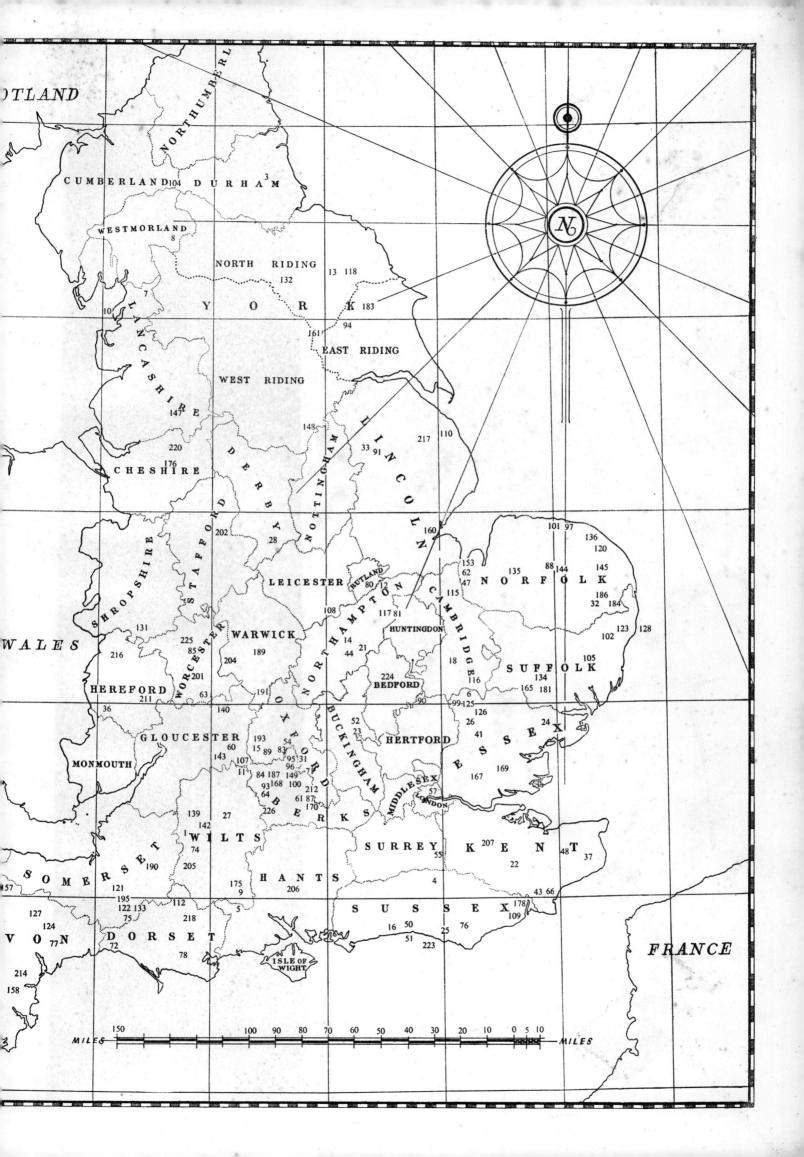